Grade 1

Addison-Wesley Mathematics

Reteaching Workbook

▲▲ **Addison-Wesley Publishing Company**

Menlo Park, California ▪ *Reading, Massachusetts* ▪ *New York*
Don Mills, Ontario ▪ *Wokingham, England* ▪ *Amsterdam* ▪ *Bonn*
Sydney ▪ *Singapore* ▪ *Tokyo* ▪ *Madrid* ▪ *San Juan*

ISBN 0-201-27107-9

3 4 5 6 7 8 9 10 - HC - 95 94 93 92 91

Table of Contents

1-1	Classification	1
1-2	My Pattern Book	2
1-3	Number Patterns to 4	3
1-4	Number Patterns to 6	4
1-5	Introduction to Problem Solving	5
1-6	Number Patterns to 9	6
1-7	Nickels and Pennies	7
1-8	Order to 9	8
1-9	Counting Before and After	9
1-10	Problem Solving	10
	Data from a Story	
2-1	Numbers 10 to 12	11
2-2	Numbers 13 to 16	12
2-3	Numbers 17 to 20	13
2-4	Dimes, Nickels, and Pennies	14
2-5	Problem Solving	15
	Understanding the Operations	
2-6	Making and Reading Graphs	16
2-7	Graphing and Comparing	17
	Numbers	
2-8	Order to 20	18
2-9	Problem Solving	19
	Retelling a Story	
3-1	Addition Expressions	20
3-2	Addition Sentences	21
3-3	My Addition Book	22
3-4	Different Ways to Show a Sum	23
3-5	Problem Solving	24
	Understanding the Operations	
3-6	Turnaround Facts and Adding 0	25
3-7	Adding in Vertical Form	26
3-8	Money Sums	27
3-9	Problem Solving	28
	Acting Out the Story	
4-1	Subtraction Expressions	29
4-2	Subtraction Sentences	30
4-3	Problem Solving	31
	Understanding the Operations	
4-4	Subtracting in Vertical Form	32
4-5	Crossing Out to Subtract	33
4-6	Zero in Subtraction	34
4-7	Related Subtraction Facts	35
4-8	Fact Families	36
4-9	Problem Solving	37
	Asking a Question	
5-1	Counting On 1 or 2	38
	and Zero Addition Facts	
5-2	Counting On	39
	with Turnaround Facts	
5-3	Counting On 3	40
5-4	Counting On 1, 2, or 3	41
5-5	Problem Solving	42
	Understanding the Operations	
5-6	Fact Practice and Probability	43
5-7	Fact Practice and Graphing	44
5-8	Problem Solving	45
	Telling a Story	
6-1	Small Doubles	46
6-2	Sums of 10	47
6-3	Fact Practice	48
6-4	Problem Solving	49
	Understanding the Operations	
6-5	Doubles Plus One	50
6-6	Fact Practice	51
6-7	Making 10, Adding Extra	52
6-8	Adding 3 Numbers	53
6-9	Problem Solving	54
	Showing Data	
7-1	Estimating and Measuring Length	55
	Nonstandard Units	
7-2	Estimating and Measuring Length	56
	Inches	
7-3	Using a Ruler Inches	57
7-4	Using a Ruler Feet	58
7-5	Ordering by Length and Height	59
7-6	Problem Solving	60
	Understanding the Operations	

7-7	Estimating and Measuring Length Centimeters	61
7-8	Estimating and Measuring Length Decimeters	62
7-9	Estimating and Measuring Weight	63
7-10	Problem Solving Is the Answer Reasonable	64
8-1	Counting Back 1 or 2	65
8-2	Counting Back 3	66
8-3	Counting Back 1, 2, or 3	67
8-4	Problem Solving Understanding the Operations	68
8-5	Zero Subtraction Facts	69
8-6	Adding to Check Subtraction	70
8-7	Subtraction Doubles	71
8-8	Fact Practice	72
8-9	Problem Solving Asking the Question	73
9-1	Sorting Solids	74
9-2	Graphing Solids	75
9-3	Plane Figures and Solids	76
9-4	Sides and Corners	77
9-5	My Geometry Book	78
9-6	Problem Solving Understanding the Operations	79
9-7	Inside, Outside, and On	80
9-8	Symmetric Figures	81
9-9	Congruent Figures	82
9-10	Problem Solving Finding the Data	83
10-1	Subtracting from 9 and 10	84
10-2	Fact Practice	85
10-3	Problem Solving Understanding the Operations	86
10-4	Counting Up to Subtract	87
10-5	Fact Practice	88
10-6	Adding to Check Subtraction	89
10-7	Fact Families	90
10-8	Fact Practice	91
10-9	Problem Solving Telling a Story	92
11-1	Grouping by Tens	93
11-2	Showing Tens and Ones	94
11-3	Decade Numbers and Names	95
11-4	Writing and Showing 2-Digit Numbers	96
11-5	Tens and Ones	97
11-6	Problem Solving Understanding the Operations	98
11-7	Trading Pennies and Dimes	99
11-8	Dimes and Pennies	100
11-9	Problem Solving Making Estimates	101
12-1	Counting to 50	102
12-2	Counting to 100	103
12-3	Counting On and Back	104
12-4	Numbers Before, After, and Between	105
12-5	Comparing Numbers	106
12-6	Problem Solving Understanding the Operations	107
12-7	Counting Patterns for 10s	108
12-8	Counting Patterns for 2s, and 5s	109
12-9	Ordinal Numbers	110
12-10	Problem Solving Finding Extra Data	111
13-1	Counting Dimes and Pennies	112
13-2	Counting Nickels and Pennies	113
13-3	Counting Dimes and Nickels	114
13-4	Counting Dimes, Nickels, and Pennies	115
13-5	Counting and Comparing Money	116
13-6	Problem Solving Understanding the Operations	117
13-7	Counting Quarters and Other Coins	118
13-8	Problem Solving Using Data from a Newspaper Ad	119
14-1	Clock Parts	120
14-2	Time on the Hour	121
14-3	Problem Solving Understanding the Operations	122
14-4	Time on the Half Hour	123
14-5	The Mouse Family's Time Book	124
14-6	Calendar	125

14-7	Problem Solving Using Data from a Chart	126
15-1	Adding with 9	127
15-2	Doubles Through 9 + 9	128
15-3	Fact Practice	129
15-4	Adding Three Numbers	130
15-5	Problem Solving Understanding the Operations	131
15-6	Doubles Plus One Through 8 + 9	132
15-7	Sums to 18	133
15-8	Fact Practice	134
15-9	Problem Solving Is the Answer Reasonable?	135
16-1	Doubles To 18	136
16-2	Subtracting 9	137
16-3	Fact Practice	138
16-4	Problem Solving Understanding the Operations	139
16-5	Using Addition to Subtract 4, 5, and 6	140
16-6	Using Addition to Subtract 7 and 8	141
16-7	Related Subtraction Facts	142
16-8	Fact Families	143
16-9	Problem Solving Using a Number Sentence	144
17-1	Counting On by Ones	145
17-2	Making a Ten	146
17-3	Problem Solving Understanding the Operations	147
17-4	Counting On by Tens	148
17-5	Adding Tens and Ones	149
17-6	Counting Back by Ones	150
17-7	Counting Back by Tens	151
17-8	Subtracting Tens and Ones	152
17-9	Problem Solving Choosing a Calculation Method	153
18-1	Multiplying Equal Groups of Two	154
18-2	Multiplying Equal Groups of Five	155
18-3	Problem Solving Understanding the Operations	156
18-4	Understanding Division Sharing	157
18-5	Understanding Division Separating	158
18-6	Fractions Halves	159
18-7	Fractions Thirds and Fourths	160
18-8	Fractions Using Sets	161
18-9	Problem Solving Finding Missing Data	162

Name _____

Classification

Ring the one that is different.

1.

2.

3.

4.

My Pattern Book

Draw to continue the pattern.

1.

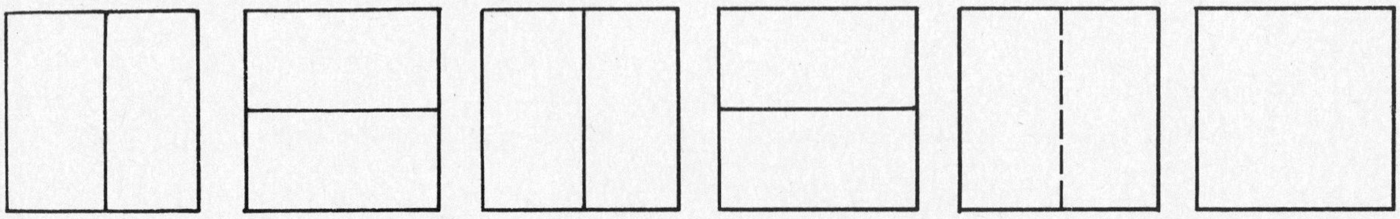

2.

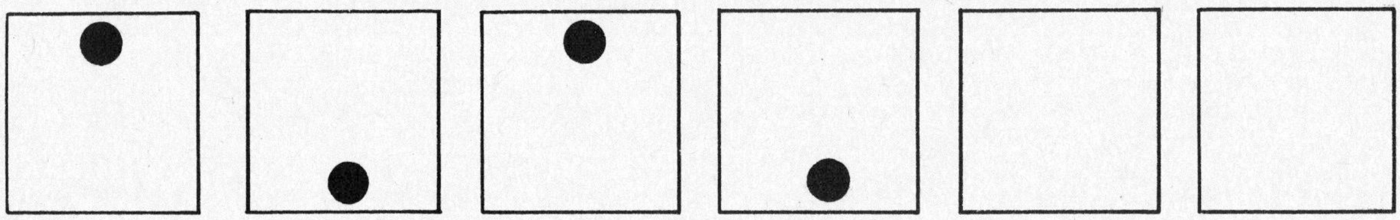

3.

4.

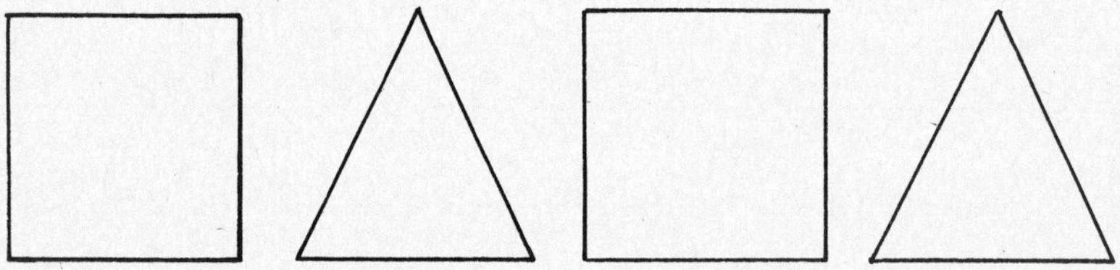

Use your red and blue ✏ . 
Color a pattern.

5.

Name _____

Number Patterns to 4

Trace the numbers with your finger.
Write the numbers.

zero

one

two

three

four

0, 1, 2, 3, 4

Write the numbers.

1.

2.

3.

4.

Name _____

Money Sums

 3¢

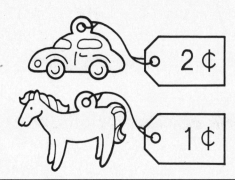 2¢

4¢

 1¢

Write how much money to pay.
Add. Ring how many pennies.

1. I buy  and .

___3___ ¢ + ___2___ ¢ = ___5___ ¢

2. I buy  and .

_____ ¢ + _____ ¢ = _____ ¢

3. I buy  and .

_____ ¢ + _____ ¢ = _____ ¢

4. I buy  and .

_____ ¢ + _____ ¢ = _____ ¢

5. I buy  and .

_____ ¢ + _____ ¢ = _____ ¢

6. I buy  and .

_____ ¢ + _____ ¢ = _____ ¢

Acting Out the Story

$$3 + 1 = 4$$

(3 bees) + (1 more bee) = (4 bees in all)

Look at the picture.
Use counters to act out the story.
Finish the number sentence.
Write the answer.

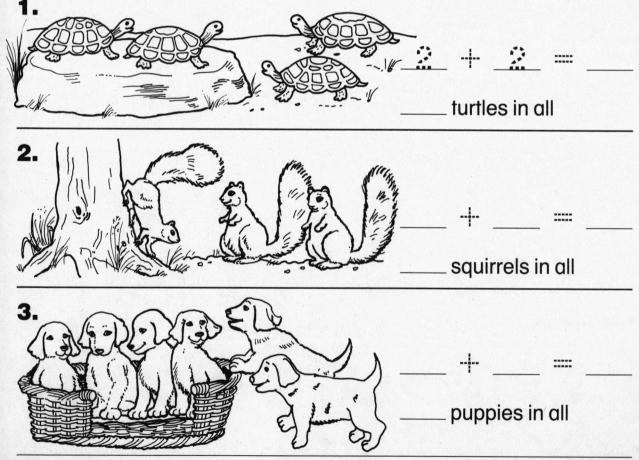

1.

$$2 + 2 = \underline{\qquad}$$

_____ turtles in all

2.

$$\underline{\qquad} + \underline{\qquad} = \underline{\qquad}$$

_____ squirrels in all

3.

$$\underline{\qquad} + \underline{\qquad} = \underline{\qquad}$$

_____ puppies in all

Name _____

Subtraction Expressions

start with   take away   are left

5   –   **2**   **3**

Write how many are left.

1.

5 – 1   ⊞
             are left

2.

6 – 2   ___
          are left

Write what you see.

3.

4 – 2   ___
        are left

4.

 3 – 1   ___
        are left

Subtraction Sentences

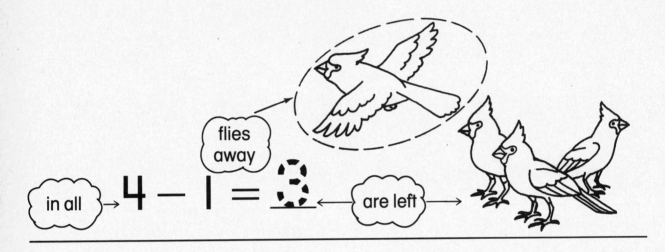

$$\text{in all} \rightarrow 4 - 1 = 3 \leftarrow \text{are left}$$

flies away

Ring the birds that fly away.
Write how many are left.

1.

$$5 - 3 = \underline{}$$

2.

$$2 - 1 = \underline{}$$

3.

$$3 - 2 = \underline{}$$

4.

$$4 - 2 = \underline{}$$

Understanding the Operations

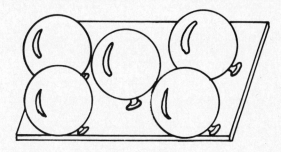 

Take away 2.

5 − 2 = 3

_5_ in all   How many are left? _3_

Solve.

1.

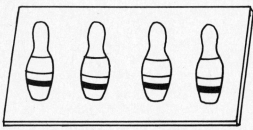 

Take away 3.

4 − 3 = ?

____ in all   How many are left? ____

2.

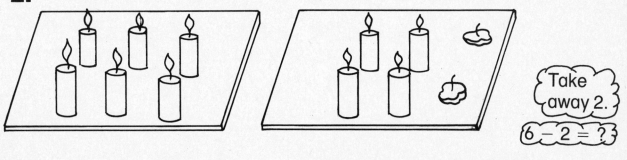

Take away 2.

6 − 2 = ?

____ in all   How many are left? ____

Subtracting in Vertical Form

Show with counters.
Subtract.

1.
$$\begin{array}{r} 3 \\ -\ 1 \\ \hline 2 \end{array}$$

(Take away 1.)

2.
$$\begin{array}{r} 5 \\ -\ 3 \\ \hline \end{array}$$

(Take away 3.)

3.
$$\begin{array}{r} 4 \\ -\ 2 \\ \hline \end{array}$$

(Take away 2.)

4.
$$\begin{array}{r} 3 \\ -\ 2 \\ \hline \end{array}$$

(Take away 2.)

5.
$$\begin{array}{r} 6 \\ -\ 1 \\ \hline \end{array}$$

(Take away 1.)

6.
$$\begin{array}{r} 4 \\ -\ 1 \\ \hline \end{array}$$

(Take away 1.)

Name _____

Crossing Out to Subtract

Show with counters.
Draw the counters.
Cross out. Subtract.

1.
$$
\begin{array}{r}
4 \\
-\,2 \\
\hline
2
\end{array}
$$

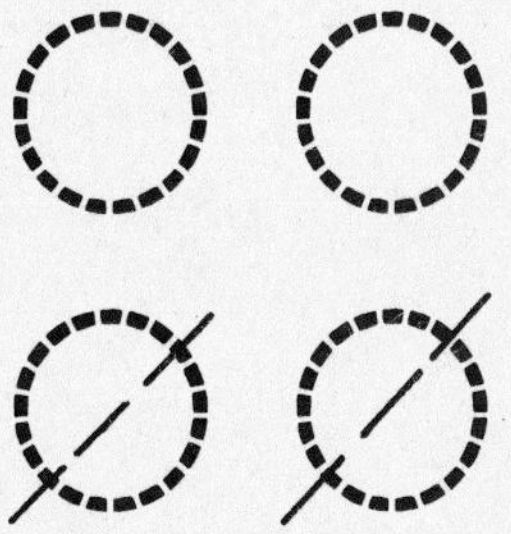

○ ○

⌀ ⌀

2.
$$
\begin{array}{r}
3 \\
-\,1 \\
\hline
\end{array}
$$

3.
$$
\begin{array}{r}
2 \\
-\,1 \\
\hline
\end{array}
$$

4.
$$
\begin{array}{r}
5 \\
-\,2 \\
\hline
\end{array}
$$

5.
$$
\begin{array}{r}
4 \\
-\,3 \\
\hline
\end{array}
$$

6.
$$
\begin{array}{r}
5 \\
-\,1 \\
\hline
\end{array}
$$

Zero in Subtraction

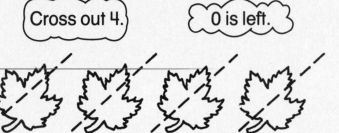

Cross out 4.   0 is left.

$$4 - 4 = \underline{0}$$

Cross out when needed. Subtract.

1.

$$3 - 3 = \underline{}$$

2.

$$5 - 0 = \underline{}$$

3.

$$4 - 0 = \underline{}$$

4.

$$5 - 5 = \underline{}$$

5.

$$3 - 0 = \underline{}$$

6.

$$2 - 2 = \underline{}$$

Name _____

Related Subtraction Facts

Cross out part.
Write how many are left.

Cross out the other part.
Write how many are left.

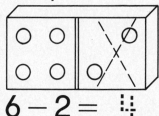

$6 - 2 = \underline{4}$

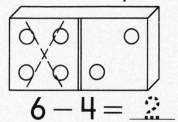

$6 - 4 = \underline{2}$

1.

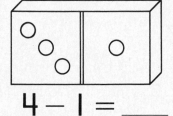

$4 - 1 = \underline{}$

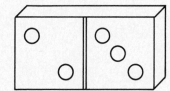

$4 - 3 = \underline{}$

2.

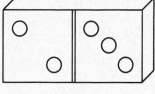

$5 - 3 = \underline{}$

$5 - 2 = \underline{}$

3.

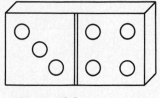

$7 - 4 = \underline{}$

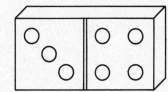

$7 - 3 = \underline{}$

Write the answer.

4. If you know $3 - 2 = 1$, you know $3 - 1 = \underline{}$.

5. If you know $6 - 1 = 5$, you know $6 - 5 = \underline{}$.

Fact Families

This is a fact family.

$2 + 1 = 3$	$3 - 2 = 1$
$1 + 2 = 3$	$3 - 1 = 2$

Add or subtract. Finish each fact family.

1.

$4 + 2 = \underline{\hspace{1cm}}$ $6 - 4 = \underline{\hspace{1cm}}$

$2 + 4 = \underline{\hspace{1cm}}$ $6 - 2 = \underline{\hspace{1cm}}$

2.

$3 + 2 = \underline{\hspace{1cm}}$ $5 - 3 = \underline{\hspace{1cm}}$

$2 + \underline{\hspace{1cm}} = \underline{\hspace{1cm}}$ $5 - 2 = \underline{\hspace{1cm}}$

Name _____

Asking a Question

Read the story.
Use counters to show it.
Ring the question that matches.
Finish the number sentence.

---

1. Three elephants | Two more join
walk. | them.

How many elephants are there in all?

How many elephants are left?   3 ◯ 2 = ____

---

2. Five seals are | One seal gets
on a rock. | off the rock.

How many seals are there in all?

How many seals are left?   5 ◯ 1 = ____

Name _____

Counting On 1 or 2 and Zero Addition Facts

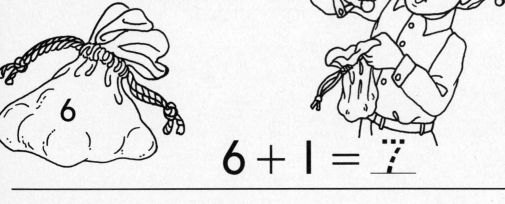

6, 7

$6 + 1 = 7$

Ring the greater number.
Add zero or count on.

1.

5   6, 7

$⑤ + 2 = 7$

8   no more

$0 + ⑧ = 8$

2. $4 + \overset{\bullet}{1} = \underline{\quad}$ ⑤ $6 + \overset{\bullet\bullet}{2} = \underline{\quad}$ $3 + 0 = \underline{\quad}$

3. $\overset{\bullet\bullet}{2} + 7 = \underline{\quad}$ $8 + \overset{\bullet}{1} = \underline{\quad}$ $0 + 6 = \underline{\quad}$

4. $5 + 0 = \underline{\quad}$ $\overset{\bullet}{1} + 5 = \underline{\quad}$ $8 + \overset{\bullet\bullet}{2} = \underline{\quad}$

5. $7 + \overset{\bullet}{1} = \underline{\quad}$ $0 + 7 = \underline{\quad}$ $\overset{\bullet\bullet}{2} + 4 = \underline{\quad}$

Counting On with Turnaround Facts

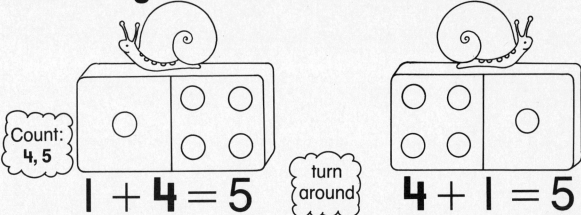

Count:
4, 5

$1 + 4 = 5$

turn around

$4 + 1 = 5$

Count on to add.
Start with the greater number.
Write the turnaround fact.

1. $3 + 2 = \underline{5}$ and $\underline{2} + \underline{3} = \underline{5}$

2. $1 + 8 = \underline{}$ and $\underline{8} + \underline{1} = \underline{}$

3. $6 + 2 = \underline{}$ and $\underline{} + \underline{} = \underline{}$

4. $4 + 3 = \underline{}$ and $\underline{} + \underline{} = \underline{}$

5. $1 + 7 = \underline{}$ and $\underline{} + \underline{} = \underline{}$

Name _____

Counting On 3

8, 9, 10

$7 + \overset{\bullet\bullet\bullet}{3} = 10$

Ring the greater number.
Count on to add.

1. $\overset{\bullet\bullet\bullet}{6} + \overset{\bullet\bullet\bullet}{3} = 9$ $\overset{\bullet\bullet\bullet}{3} + \overset{}{5} = \underline{\quad}$ $\overset{\bullet\bullet\bullet}{4} + \overset{\bullet\bullet\bullet}{3} = \underline{\quad}$

7, 8, 9   6, 7, 8   5, 6, 7

2. $\overset{\bullet\bullet\bullet}{3} + 8 = \underline{\quad}$ $9 + \overset{\bullet\bullet\bullet}{3} = \underline{\quad}$ $5 + \overset{\bullet\bullet\bullet}{3} = \underline{\quad}$

9, 10, 11   10, 11, 12   6, 7, 8

3. $\overset{\bullet\bullet\bullet}{3} + 8 = \underline{\quad}$ $\overset{\bullet\bullet\bullet}{3} + 7 = \underline{\quad}$ $\overset{\bullet\bullet\bullet}{3} + 9 = \underline{\quad}$

4. $7 + \overset{\bullet\bullet\bullet}{3} = \underline{\quad}$ $\overset{\bullet\bullet\bullet}{3} + 6 = \underline{\quad}$ $\overset{\bullet\bullet\bullet}{3} + 4 = \underline{\quad}$

Counting On 1, 2, or 3

Ring the greater number.
Then count on to find the sum.

1.
$$\begin{array}{r} 2 \\ +\enclose{circle}{5} \\ \hline 7 \end{array}$$
Count on 2.
6, 7

$$\begin{array}{r} \enclose{circle}{7} \\ +1 \\ \hline \end{array}$$

Count on 3.
5, 6, 7
$$\begin{array}{r} \enclose{circle}{4} \\ +3 \\ \hline \end{array}$$

Count on 1. **8**

2.
$$\begin{array}{r} 2 \\ +\enclose{circle}{6} \\ \hline \end{array}$$
$$\begin{array}{r} \enclose{circle}{6} \\ +1 \\ \hline \end{array}$$
$$\begin{array}{r} \enclose{circle}{7} \\ +3 \\ \hline \end{array}$$
$$\begin{array}{r} 2 \\ +\enclose{circle}{4} \\ \hline \end{array}$$
$$\begin{array}{r} 8 \\ +\enclose{circle}{3} \\ \hline \end{array}$$

3.
$$\begin{array}{r} 8 \\ +2 \\ \hline \end{array}$$
$$\begin{array}{r} 3 \\ +5 \\ \hline \end{array}$$
$$\begin{array}{r} 1 \\ +9 \\ \hline \end{array}$$
$$\begin{array}{r} 9 \\ +2 \\ \hline \end{array}$$
$$\begin{array}{r} 5 \\ +1 \\ \hline \end{array}$$

4.
$$\begin{array}{r} 2 \\ +7 \\ \hline \end{array}$$
$$\begin{array}{r} 4 \\ +1 \\ \hline \end{array}$$
$$\begin{array}{r} 6 \\ +3 \\ \hline \end{array}$$
$$\begin{array}{r} 4 \\ +2 \\ \hline \end{array}$$
$$\begin{array}{r} 9 \\ +3 \\ \hline \end{array}$$

5.
$$\begin{array}{r} 2 \\ +9 \\ \hline \end{array}$$
$$\begin{array}{r} 3 \\ +8 \\ \hline \end{array}$$
$$\begin{array}{r} 5 \\ +2 \\ \hline \end{array}$$
$$\begin{array}{r} 9 \\ +1 \\ \hline \end{array}$$
$$\begin{array}{r} 1 \\ +8 \\ \hline \end{array}$$

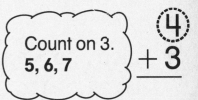

Name _____

Understanding the Operations

Solve. Use the pictures to help.
Finish the number sentence.

Cross out the 3 marbles Lisa gave away.

1. Lisa had 5 marbles.
She gave away 3.
How many left? 〈Subtract.〉 5 ⊖ 3 = ____

2. Gary found 3 cans.
Rob found 3 cans.
How many did they find together?
〈Add.〉 3 ◯ 3 = ____

3. Jamal saw 2 ducks.
Then 4 more ducks came.
How many ducks did he see?

2 ◯ 4 = ____

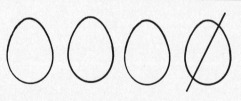

4. Paola had 4 eggs.
Then she broke 1 of them.
How many does she have left?

4 ◯ 1 = ____

Fact Practice and Probability

7, 8

$$6 + 2 = \underline{\quad}$$

6

Ring the greater number.
Count on to add.

1. ⑧ $+ 1 = \underline{9}$ $\ddot{2} + ⑤ = \underline{\quad}$ $\dddot{3} + ⑧ = \underline{\quad}$

9   6, 7   9, 10, 11

2. $7 + \dot{1} = \underline{\quad}$ $0 + 6 = \underline{\quad}$ $4 + \ddot{2} = \underline{\quad}$

8   5, 6

3. $\ddot{2} + 3 = \underline{\quad}$ $4 + \dot{1} = \underline{\quad}$ $\dddot{3} + 6 = \underline{\quad}$

4. $5 + \dot{1} = \underline{\quad}$ $7 + 0 = \underline{\quad}$ $\ddot{2} + 8 = \underline{\quad}$

Fact Practice

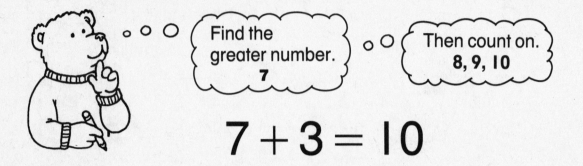

Find the greater number.
7

Then count on.
8, 9, 10

$$7 + 3 = 10$$

Ring the greater number.
Count on to add.

1. $2 + ⑦ = \underline{9}$ $⑧ + 3 = \underline{}$ $3 + ⑥ = \underline{}$

2. $5 + 1 = \underline{}$ $3 + 9 = \underline{}$ $8 + 2 = \underline{}$

3. $6 + 2 = \underline{}$ $2 + 5 = \underline{}$ $9 + 2 = \underline{}$

4. $3 + 4 = \underline{}$ $7 + 2 = \underline{}$ $3 + 5 = \underline{}$

5. $9 + 3 = \underline{}$ $6 + 1 = \underline{}$ $6 + 3 = \underline{}$

Name _____

Telling a Story

Tell a story about the picture.
Finish the number sentence for the story.

1.

$$\underline{3} + \underline{4} = \underline{}$$

2.

$$\underline{2} - \underline{} = \underline{}$$

3.

$$\underline{} - \underline{} = \underline{}$$

4.

$$\underline{} + \underline{} = \underline{}$$

Small Doubles

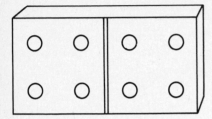 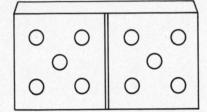 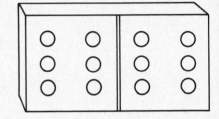

$$4 + 4 = \underline{8} \qquad 5 + 5 = \underline{10} \qquad 6 + 6 = \underline{12}$$

Add. Look for doubles facts.

1.
$$\begin{array}{r} 6 \\ +1 \\ \hline 7 \end{array} \qquad \begin{array}{r} 4 \\ +4 \\ \hline \end{array} \qquad \begin{array}{r} 2 \\ +4 \\ \hline \end{array} \qquad \begin{array}{r} 5 \\ +5 \\ \hline \end{array} \qquad \begin{array}{r} 3 \\ +3 \\ \hline \end{array}$$

2.
$$\begin{array}{r} 6 \\ +6 \\ \hline \end{array} \qquad \begin{array}{r} 7 \\ +3 \\ \hline \end{array} \qquad \begin{array}{r} 2 \\ +2 \\ \hline \end{array} \qquad \begin{array}{r} 9 \\ +2 \\ \hline \end{array} \qquad \begin{array}{r} 4 \\ +4 \\ \hline \end{array}$$

3.
$$\begin{array}{r} 5 \\ +5 \\ \hline \end{array} \qquad \begin{array}{r} 2 \\ +6 \\ \hline \end{array} \qquad \begin{array}{r} 2 \\ +8 \\ \hline \end{array} \qquad \begin{array}{r} 6 \\ +6 \\ \hline \end{array} \qquad \begin{array}{r} 1 \\ +1 \\ \hline \end{array}$$

Now, ring all the doubles.

Sums of 10

This is a sum of 10.

$$\begin{array}{r} 6 \\ +\ 4 \\ \hline 10 \end{array}$$

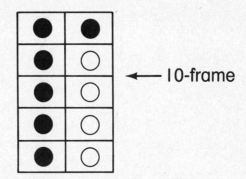

← 10-frame

Add. Use counters and a 10-frame.
Ring sums of 10.

1.

$$\begin{array}{r} 9 \\ +\ 1 \\ \hline 10 \end{array}$$

$$\begin{array}{r} 5 \\ +\ 2 \\ \hline \end{array}$$

$$\begin{array}{r} 3 \\ +\ 6 \\ \hline \end{array}$$

$$\begin{array}{r} 8 \\ +\ 2 \\ \hline \end{array}$$

2.

$$\begin{array}{r} 4 \\ +\ 6 \\ \hline \end{array}$$

$$\begin{array}{r} 5 \\ +\ 5 \\ \hline \end{array}$$

$$\begin{array}{r} 3 \\ +\ 8 \\ \hline \end{array}$$

$$\begin{array}{r} 6 \\ +\ 6 \\ \hline \end{array}$$

3.

$$\begin{array}{r} 7 \\ +\ 2 \\ \hline \end{array}$$

$$\begin{array}{r} 2 \\ +\ 8 \\ \hline \end{array}$$

$$\begin{array}{r} 5 \\ +\ 6 \\ \hline \end{array}$$

$$\begin{array}{r} 3 \\ +\ 7 \\ \hline \end{array}$$

Fact Practice

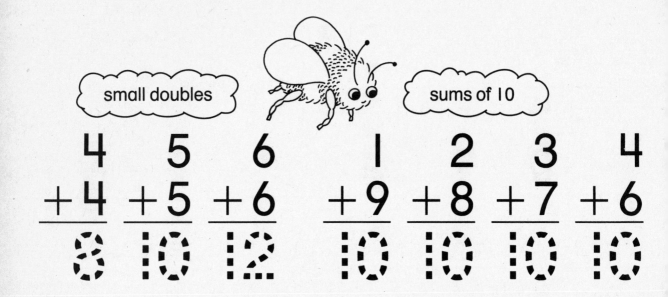

small doubles   sums of 10

$$
\begin{array}{cccccccc}
4 & 5 & 6 & 1 & 2 & 3 & 4 \\
+4 & +5 & +6 & +9 & +8 & +7 & +6 \\
\hline
8 & 10 & 12 & 10 & 10 & 10 & 10
\end{array}
$$

1. Add. Ring sums of 8.

$$
\begin{array}{ccccc}
5 & 6 & 6 & 1 & 8 \\
+3 & +3 & +1 & +7 & +0 \\
\hline
8 & & & &
\end{array}
$$

2. Add. Ring sums of 12.

$$
\begin{array}{ccccc}
2 & 6 & 3 & 9 & 9 \\
+7 & +6 & +9 & +2 & +1 \\
\hline
\end{array}
$$

3. Add. Ring sums of 10.

$$
\begin{array}{ccccc}
1 & 3 & 5 & 6 & 3 \\
+9 & +4 & +5 & +3 & +7 \\
\hline
\end{array}
$$

Understanding the Operations

2 + 5 = 7 (in all)

(this means put together)

Use counters to show each group.
Put together the two groups.
Finish the number sentence.

1. 4 ⊕ 2 = 6
in all

2. 8 ◯ 1 = _____
in all

3. 5 ◯ 5 = _____
in all

4. 6 ◯ 2 = _____
in all

Doubles Plus One

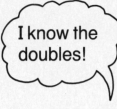

I know the doubles!

Then these should be easy.

$1 + 1 = 2$

$2 + 2 = 4$

$3 + 3 = 6$

$4 + 4 = 8$

$5 + 5 = 10$

$6 + 6 = 12$

$1 + 2 = \underline{3}$

$2 + 3 = \underline{}$

$3 + 4 = \underline{}$

$4 + 5 = \underline{}$

$5 + 6 = \underline{}$

Add.

1.
$$\begin{array}{r} 7 \\ +2 \\ \hline \end{array} \qquad \begin{array}{r} 5 \\ +5 \\ \hline \end{array} \qquad \begin{array}{r} 3 \\ +2 \\ \hline \end{array} \qquad \begin{array}{r} 4 \\ +3 \\ \hline \end{array} \qquad \begin{array}{r} 2 \\ +2 \\ \hline \end{array}$$

2.
$$\begin{array}{r} 4 \\ +4 \\ \hline \end{array} \qquad \begin{array}{r} 4 \\ +5 \\ \hline \end{array} \qquad \begin{array}{r} 3 \\ +3 \\ \hline \end{array} \qquad \begin{array}{r} 8 \\ +2 \\ \hline \end{array} \qquad \begin{array}{r} 6 \\ +6 \\ \hline \end{array}$$

Ring doubles red.

Ring doubles plus one green.

Fact Practice

Ring the <u>doubles</u> blue.
Ring the <u>doubles plus one</u> red.
Then add.

B	R	R	B
4	4	5	3
+4	+5	+4	+3
8	9		

4 + 4 = 8, 1 more!

R	R	B	R
5	3	5	6
+6	+4	+5	+5

5 + 5 = 10, 1 more

Add.

1.

7	6	4	6	6
+2	+6	+5	+4	+5

2.

3	4	1	5	4
+8	+6	+9	+6	+4

Making 10, Adding Extra

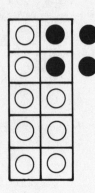

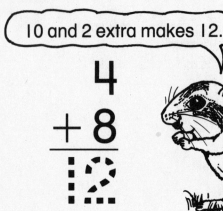

8
+4
‾‾‾
12

4
+8
‾‾‾
12

10 and 2 extra makes 12.

Draw 4 ○ and 7 ●.
Add.

1.

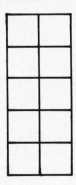

4
+7
‾‾‾

7
+4
‾‾‾

Draw 4 ○ and 8 ●.
Add.

2.

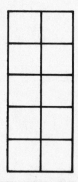

4
+8
‾‾‾

8
+4
‾‾‾

Draw 7 ○ and 5 ●.
Add.

3.

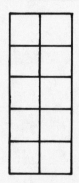

7
+5
‾‾‾

5
+7
‾‾‾

Adding 3 Numbers

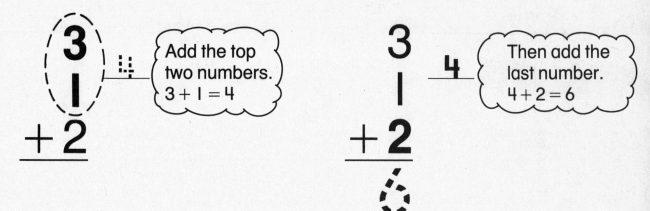

Add.

1.
```
  3
  2
 +2
 ___
  7
```
5   (5 + 2 = 7)

```
  2
  4
 +2
 ___
```
6   (6 + 2 = ?)

```
  4
  3
 +3
 ___
```
7   (7 + 3 = ?)

2.
```
  6
  2
 +3
 ___
```
___

```
  3
  5
 +2
 ___
```
___

```
  6
  3
 +3
 ___
```
___

3.
```
  4
  4
 +4
 ___
```
___

```
  7
  2
 +1
 ___
```
___

```
  4
  5
 +2
 ___
```
___

Showing Data

3 bees fly.
I bee joins them.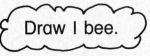

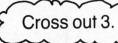 Draw I bee.
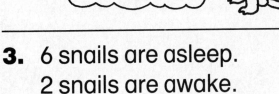

4 bees fly.
2 bees stop.

Cross out
2 bees.

Read the story. Draw more pictures or cross out some.

1. 6 frogs swim.
4 frogs join them.

Draw 4 more.

2. 9 turtles walk.
3 sit down.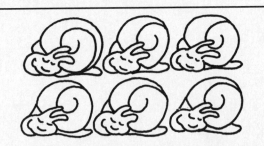

Cross out 3.

3. 6 snails are asleep.
2 snails are awake.

Draw more.

4. 7 worms fish.
3 worms go for a walk.

Name _____

Estimating and Measuring Length: Nonstandard Units

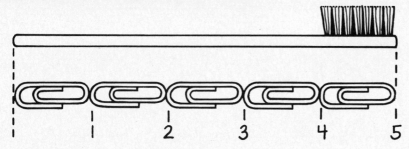

1	2	3	4	5

Guess how many clips.
Count to find the length.

1.

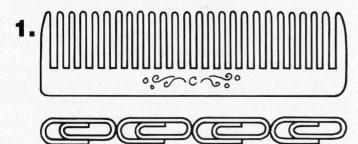

guess _____

count _____

2.

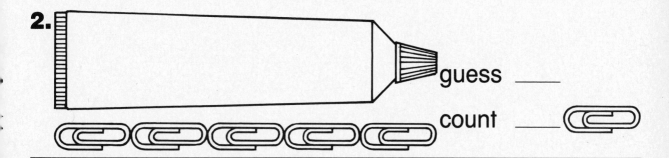

guess _____

count _____

3.

guess _____

count _____

Name _____

Estimating and Measuring Length: Inches

Make an inch strip like this.
Line up the edge of the inch strip
on the black line. Measure.

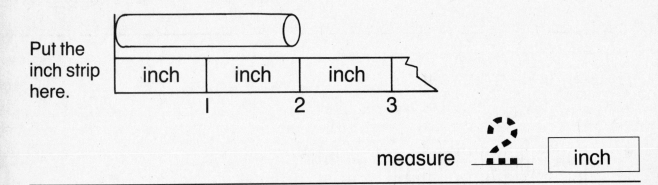

Put the
inch strip
here.

inch	inch	inch

1   2   3

measure _____ | inch |

_____

Estimate.
Then measure with your inch strip.

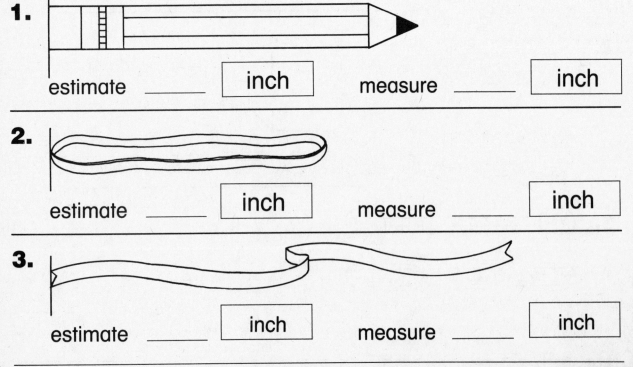

1.

estimate _____ | inch | measure _____ | inch |

_____

2.

estimate _____ | inch | measure _____ | inch |

_____

3.

estimate _____ | inch | measure _____ | inch |

Name _____

Using a Ruler: Inches

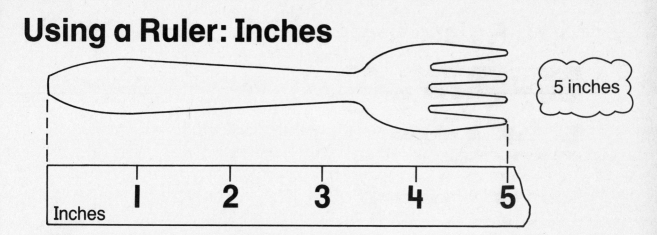

5 inches

Use your punchout inch ruler.
Measure. Write the length.

1.

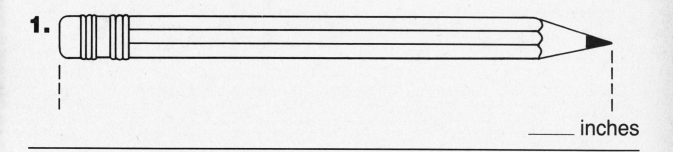

_____ inches

2.

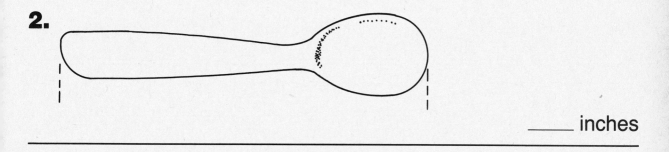

_____ inches

3.

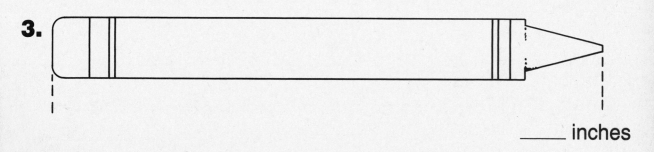

_____ inches

Name _____

Using a Ruler: Feet

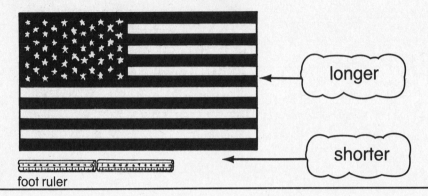

longer

shorter

foot ruler

Ring **longer** or **shorter**.

1.

The  is
longer.
 ⟨shorter.⟩

2.

The  is
longer.

shorter.

3.

The ▭ is
longer.

shorter.

4.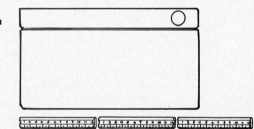

The 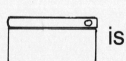 is
longer.

shorter.

Ordering by Length and Height

These strings are in order
from shortest to longest.

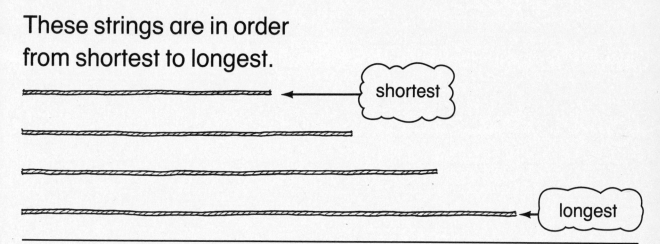

shortest

longest

Color the longest or tallest green.
Color the shortest yellow.

1.
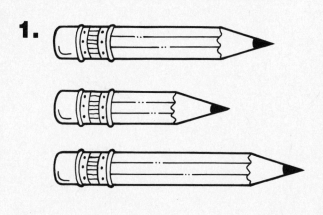

2.

3.

4.
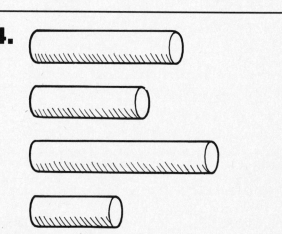

Understanding the Operations

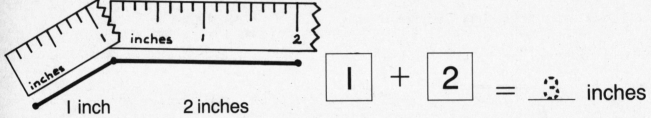

$$\boxed{1} + \boxed{2} = \underline{} \text{ inches}$$

1 inch   2 inches

Use your inch ruler.
Find the length of each path.

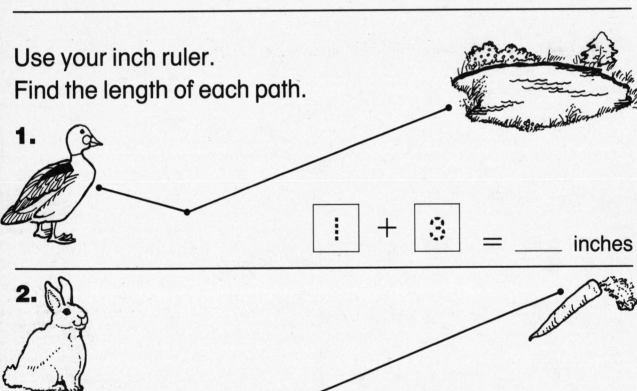

1.

$$\boxed{} + \boxed{} = \underline{} \text{ inches}$$

2.

$$\boxed{} + \boxed{} = \underline{} \text{ inches}$$

3.

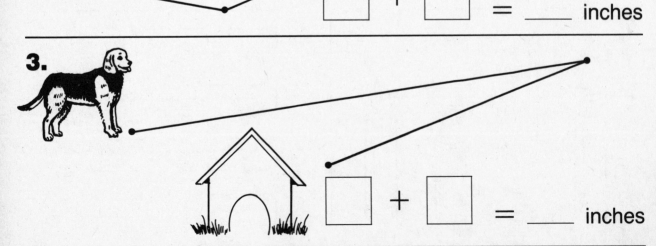

$$\boxed{} + \boxed{} = \underline{} \text{ inches}$$

Estimating and Measuring Length: Centimeters

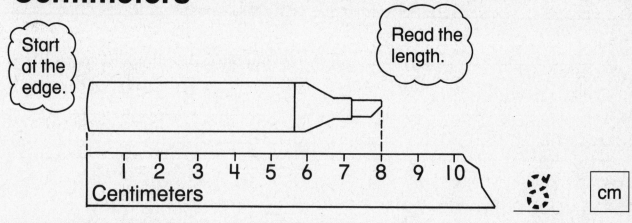

Start at the edge.

Read the length.

Centimeters
1 2 3 4 5 6 7 8 9 10

8 cm

Use your punchout centimeter ruler.
Measure.

Read the length.

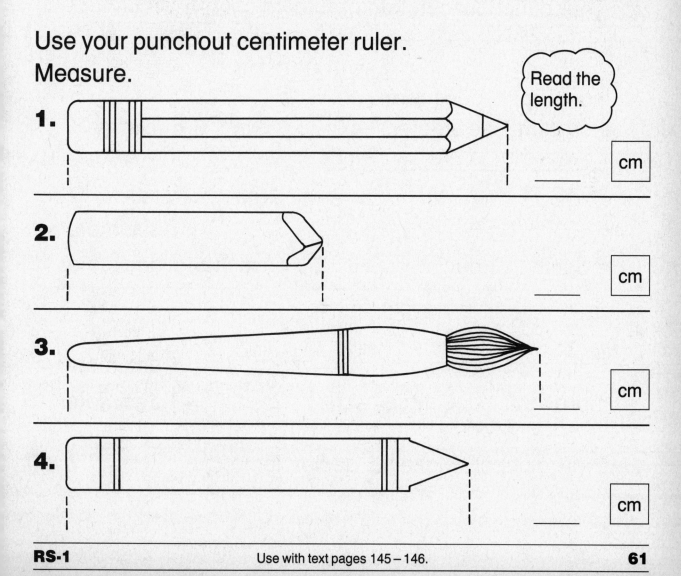

1. _____ cm

2. _____ cm

3. _____ cm

4. _____ cm

Name _____

Estimating and Measuring Length: Decimeters

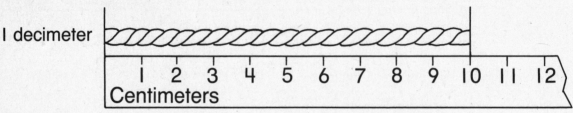

I decimeter

Centimeters

I decimeter is the same as 10 centimeters.

Ring your estimate.
Use your punchout centimeter ruler to check.

1.

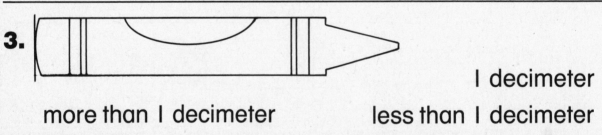

more than I decimeter
less than I decimeter   I decimeter

2.

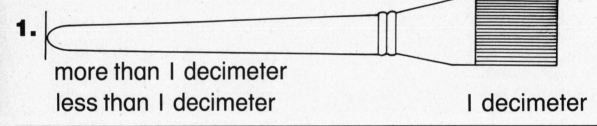

I decimeter
more than I decimeter   less than I decimeter

3.

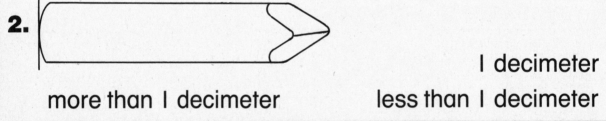

I decimeter
more than I decimeter   less than I decimeter

4. Draw a pencil. Make it I decimeter long.

Name _____

Estimating and Measuring Capacity

Work with a partner.
Look at these cups filled with juice.

This cup is filled.   This cup is not filled.

Tell why the second cup is not filled.
Talk about it with your partner.

Color to show how many cups each will fill.

1.

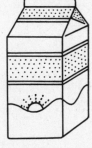

holds 4 cups

2.

holds 2 cups

Name _____

Determining Reasonable Answers

This crayon is 5 centimeters.

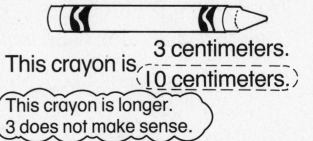

This crayon is, 3 centimeters.
10 centimeters.

This crayon is longer.
3 does not make sense.

Ring the answer that makes sense.

1.

This puppy weighs 5 pounds.

How much does this puppy weigh?

4 pounds   8 pounds

2.

Maria is 4 feet tall.

How tall is Cary?

3 feet   5 feet

3.

This bottle fills 6 cups.

How many cups does this bottle fill?

9 cups   4 cups

Counting Back 1 or 2

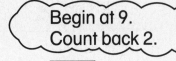
Begin at 9.
Count back 2.

⬚ 9   8, 7 $9 - 2 = 7$

Count back to subtract.

1. $6 - 2 = 4$ $10 - 1 = \_\_$ $8 - 2 = \_\_$
      5, 4   9   7, 6

2. $11 - 2 = \_\_$ $7 - 1 = \_\_$ $9 - 1 = \_\_$
      10, 9   6   8

3. $10 - 2 = \_\_$ $5 - 1 = \_\_$ $4 - 2 = \_\_$

4. $8 - 1 = \_\_$ $7 - 2 = \_\_$ $5 - 2 = \_\_$

5. $6 - 1 = \_\_$ $4 - 1 = \_\_$ $3 - 2 = \_\_$

Counting Back 3

Count back to subtract.
Draw the jumps.

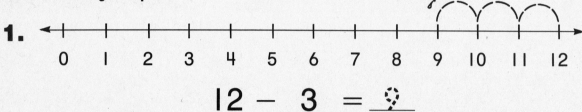

1.

| | | | | | | | | | | | | |
|0|1|2|3|4|5|6|7|8|9|10|11|12|

$$12 - 3 = \underline{9}$$
start jump end
back

2.

| | | | | | | | | | | | | |
|0|1|2|3|4|5|6|7|8|9|10|11|12|

$$10 - 3 = \underline{\quad}$$
start jump end
back

3.

| | | | | | | | | | | | | |
|0|1|2|3|4|5|6|7|8|9|10|11|12|

$$11 - 3 = \underline{\quad}$$
start jump end
back

4.

| | | | | | | | | | | | | |
|0|1|2|3|4|5|6|7|8|9|10|11|12|

$$9 - 3 = \underline{\quad}$$
start jump end
back

Name _____

Counting Back I, 2, or 3

Count back 3.

7, 6, 5

8

$8 - 3 = 5$

Count back I, 2, or 3 to subtract.

1. $10 - \overset{..}{2} = 8$ $6 - \overset{...}{3} = \rule{1cm}{0.4pt}$ $11 - \overset{...}{3} = \rule{1cm}{0.4pt}$

9, 8   5, 4, 3   10, 9, 8

2. $9 - \overset{...}{3} = \rule{1cm}{0.4pt}$ $11 - \overset{..}{2} = \rule{1cm}{0.4pt}$ $10 - \overset{...}{3} = \rule{1cm}{0.4pt}$

8, 7, 6   10, 9   9, 8, 7

3. $10 - \overset{..}{2} = \rule{1cm}{0.4pt}$ $5 - \overset{.}{1} = \rule{1cm}{0.4pt}$ $4 - \overset{..}{2} = \rule{1cm}{0.4pt}$

4. $5 - 3 = \rule{1cm}{0.4pt}$ $9 - 2 = \rule{1cm}{0.4pt}$ $10 - 1 = \rule{1cm}{0.4pt}$

5. $7 - 2 = \rule{1cm}{0.4pt}$ $12 - 3 = \rule{1cm}{0.4pt}$ $5 - 1 = \rule{1cm}{0.4pt}$

RS-1   Use with text pages 161–162.   **67**

Understanding the Operations

Write the number sentence.
Use the picture to help.

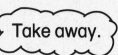
Take away.

1. 6 birds on the pole.
2 fly away.
How many birds still on the pole?

___6___ (──) ___2___ ═══ _____

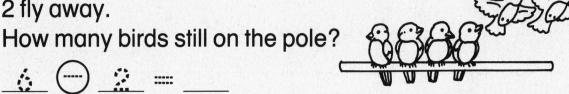

Compare.

2. 5 acorns on top.
3 acorns below.
How many more acorns on top?

_____ ◯ _____ ═══ _____

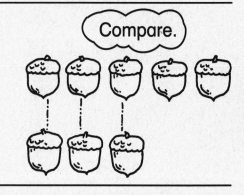

3. 7 puppies playing.
I puppy sits down.
How many puppies did not sit down?

_____ ◯ _____ ═══ _____

4. 8 crayons on the table.
3 pencils on the table.
How many more crayons than pencils?

_____ ◯ _____ ═══ _____

Zero Subtraction Facts

These are zero facts.

$$\begin{array}{r} 4 \\ -\ 4 \\ \hline 0 \end{array}$$

$$\begin{array}{r} 4 \\ -\ 0 \\ \hline 4 \end{array}$$

Take away all. Zero are left.

Take away zero. All are left.

Look for the zero facts. Ring them.
Subtract.

1.

$$\begin{array}{r} 6 \\ -\ 6 \\ \hline 0 \end{array}$$

$$\begin{array}{r} 7 \\ -\ 2 \\ \hline \end{array}$$

$$\begin{array}{r} 7 \\ -\ 0 \\ \hline \end{array}$$

$$\begin{array}{r} 2 \\ -\ 2 \\ \hline \end{array}$$

$$\begin{array}{r} 8 \\ -\ 1 \\ \hline \end{array}$$

2.

$$\begin{array}{r} 10 \\ -\ 2 \\ \hline \end{array}$$

$$\begin{array}{r} 1 \\ -\ 0 \\ \hline \end{array}$$

$$\begin{array}{r} 8 \\ -\ 3 \\ \hline \end{array}$$

$$\begin{array}{r} 7 \\ -\ 7 \\ \hline \end{array}$$

$$\begin{array}{r} 8 \\ -\ 0 \\ \hline \end{array}$$

3.

$$\begin{array}{r} 6 \\ -\ 2 \\ \hline \end{array}$$

$$\begin{array}{r} 7 \\ -\ 3 \\ \hline \end{array}$$

$$\begin{array}{r} 5 \\ -\ 0 \\ \hline \end{array}$$

$$\begin{array}{r} 9 \\ -\ 9 \\ \hline \end{array}$$

$$\begin{array}{r} 1 \\ -\ 1 \\ \hline \end{array}$$

4.

$$\begin{array}{r} 6 \\ -\ 0 \\ \hline \end{array}$$

$$\begin{array}{r} 9 \\ -\ 2 \\ \hline \end{array}$$

$$\begin{array}{r} 11 \\ -\ 2 \\ \hline \end{array}$$

$$\begin{array}{r} 9 \\ -\ 0 \\ \hline \end{array}$$

$$\begin{array}{r} 5 \\ -\ 5 \\ \hline \end{array}$$

Adding to Check Subtraction

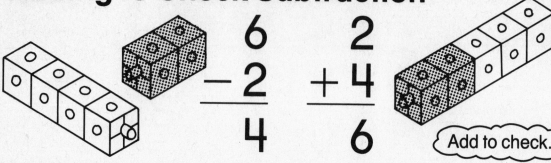

$$\begin{array}{r} 6 \\ -2 \\ \hline 4 \end{array} \qquad \begin{array}{r} 2 \\ +4 \\ \hline 6 \end{array}$$

Add to check.

Subtract.

Then add to check.

Use cubes to show what you do.

1.

$$\begin{array}{r} 4 \\ -\boxed{\vdots} \\ \hline \bigodot \end{array} \qquad \begin{array}{r} \boxed{\vdots} \\ +\bigodot \\ \hline \boxed{4} \end{array} \qquad \begin{array}{r} 5 \\ -\boxed{3} \\ \hline \bigcirc \end{array} \qquad \begin{array}{r} \boxed{3} \\ +\bigcirc \\ \hline \end{array}$$

Subtract. Finish the add-to-check fact.

2.

$$\begin{array}{r} 7 \\ -\boxed{3} \\ \hline \bigcirc \end{array} \begin{array}{r} \boxed{3} \\ +\bigcirc \\ \hline \end{array} \qquad \begin{array}{r} 4 \\ -\boxed{0} \\ \hline \bigcirc \end{array} \begin{array}{r} \boxed{0} \\ +\bigcirc \\ \hline \end{array} \qquad \begin{array}{r} 5 \\ -\boxed{4} \\ \hline \bigcirc \end{array} \begin{array}{r} \boxed{4} \\ +\bigcirc \\ \hline \end{array}$$

3.

$$\begin{array}{r} 12 \\ -9 \\ \hline \end{array} \begin{array}{r} 9 \\ +\boxed{} \\ \hline \end{array} \qquad \begin{array}{r} 10 \\ -5 \\ \hline \end{array} \begin{array}{r} 5 \\ +\boxed{} \\ \hline \end{array} \qquad \begin{array}{r} 9 \\ -3 \\ \hline \end{array} \begin{array}{r} 3 \\ +\boxed{} \\ \hline \end{array}$$

Subtraction Doubles

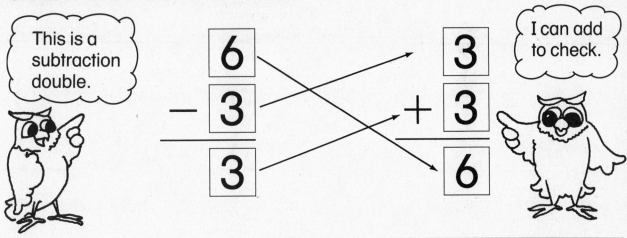

This is a subtraction double.

I can add to check.

$$
\begin{array}{r} 6 \\ -\ 3 \\ \hline 3 \end{array}
\qquad
\begin{array}{r} 3 \\ +\ 3 \\ \hline 6 \end{array}
$$

You need two sets of number cards 1 – 12, 12 counters, and a partner. Arrange your cards to show the subtraction. Your partner moves the cards to show the add-to-check fact. Use counters to check. Write the missing numbers.

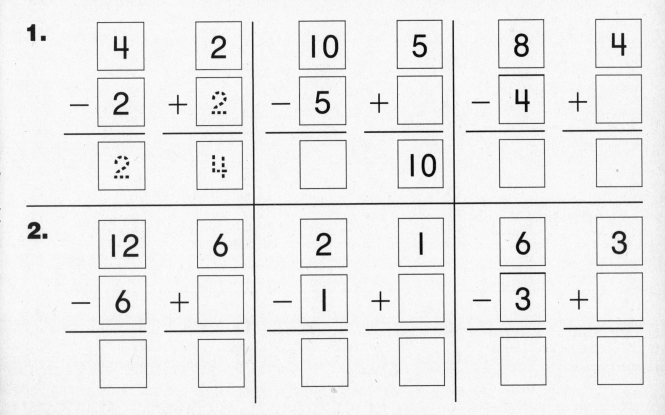

1.

$$
\begin{array}{r} 4 \\ -\ 2 \\ \hline 2 \end{array}
\quad
\begin{array}{r} 2 \\ +\ 2 \\ \hline 4 \end{array}
\qquad
\begin{array}{r} 10 \\ -\ 5 \\ \hline \ \end{array}
\quad
\begin{array}{r} 5 \\ +\ \ \\ \hline 10 \end{array}
\qquad
\begin{array}{r} 8 \\ -\ 4 \\ \hline \ \end{array}
\quad
\begin{array}{r} 4 \\ +\ \ \\ \hline \ \end{array}
$$

2.

$$
\begin{array}{r} 12 \\ -\ 6 \\ \hline \ \end{array}
\quad
\begin{array}{r} 6 \\ +\ \ \\ \hline \ \end{array}
\qquad
\begin{array}{r} 2 \\ -\ 1 \\ \hline \ \end{array}
\quad
\begin{array}{r} 1 \\ +\ \ \\ \hline \ \end{array}
\qquad
\begin{array}{r} 6 \\ -\ 3 \\ \hline \ \end{array}
\quad
\begin{array}{r} 3 \\ +\ \ \\ \hline \ \end{array}
$$

Name _____

Fact Practice

$$\begin{array}{r} 10 \\ -1 \\ \hline 9 \end{array} \qquad \begin{array}{r} 9 \\ -3 \\ \hline 6 \end{array} \qquad \begin{array}{r} 7 \\ -0 \\ \hline 7 \end{array} \qquad \begin{array}{r} 5 \\ -5 \\ \hline 0 \end{array} \qquad \begin{array}{r} 8 \\ -4 \\ \hline 4 \end{array} \qquad \begin{array}{r} 2 \\ -1 \\ \hline 1 \end{array}$$

count back facts   zero facts   doubles

Subtract.

1. count back facts
$$\begin{array}{r} 10 \\ -3 \\ \hline \end{array} \qquad \begin{array}{r} 7 \\ -1 \\ \hline \end{array} \qquad \begin{array}{r} 9 \\ -2 \\ \hline \end{array} \qquad \begin{array}{r} 6 \\ -3 \\ \hline \end{array} \qquad \begin{array}{r} 8 \\ -1 \\ \hline \end{array}$$

2. zero facts
$$\begin{array}{r} 9 \\ -0 \\ \hline \end{array} \qquad \begin{array}{r} 6 \\ -6 \\ \hline \end{array} \qquad \begin{array}{r} 4 \\ -0 \\ \hline \end{array} \qquad \begin{array}{r} 8 \\ -0 \\ \hline \end{array} \qquad \begin{array}{r} 7 \\ -7 \\ \hline \end{array}$$

3. doubles
$$\begin{array}{r} 6 \\ -3 \\ \hline \end{array} \qquad \begin{array}{r} 4 \\ -2 \\ \hline \end{array} \qquad \begin{array}{r} 12 \\ -6 \\ \hline \end{array} \qquad \begin{array}{r} 8 \\ -4 \\ \hline \end{array} \qquad \begin{array}{r} 10 \\ -5 \\ \hline \end{array}$$

4.
$$\begin{array}{r} 8 \\ -2 \\ \hline \end{array} \qquad \begin{array}{r} 12 \\ -6 \\ \hline \end{array} \qquad \begin{array}{r} 9 \\ -1 \\ \hline \end{array} \qquad \begin{array}{r} 6 \\ -0 \\ \hline \end{array} \qquad \begin{array}{r} 11 \\ -2 \\ \hline \end{array} \qquad \begin{array}{r} 12 \\ -3 \\ \hline \end{array}$$

Name _____

Asking the Question

Ring the best question for each story.
Use the picture to help.

1. Gary had 6 rocks in his box.
He lost 2 rocks.

⟨How many rocks are left in his box?⟩

How many rocks are there?

---

2. 5 white rabbits playing in the yard.
3 black rabbits hopped in to play.

How many rabbits are there in all?

How many rabbits are left?

---

3. 7 horses were in the field.
3 horses ran back to the barn.

How many horses are left in the field?

How many horses are there?

Sorting Solids

Draw lines to match.

The ball is a sphere shape. It is round and shaped like a sphere.

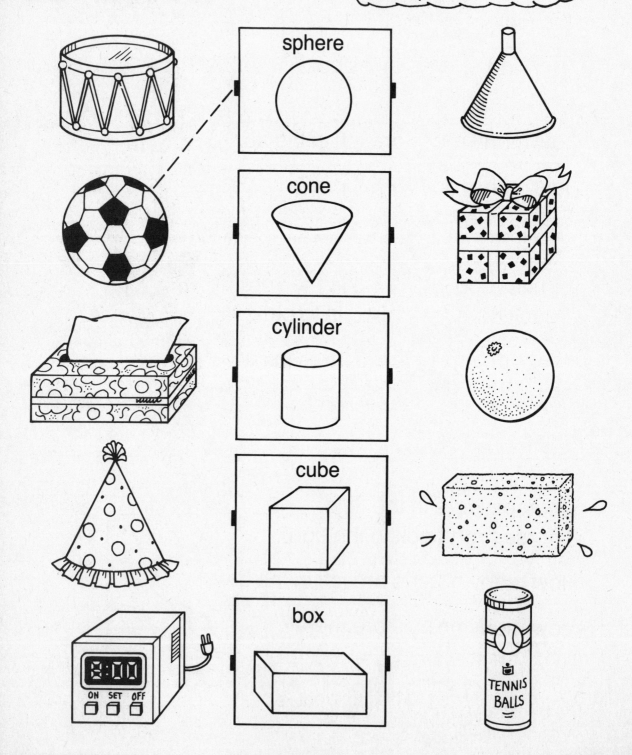

sphere

cone

cylinder

cube

box

Name _____

Graphing Solids

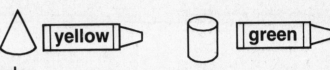

Color a ☐ on the graph
for each solid you find.
Color each solid as you graph.

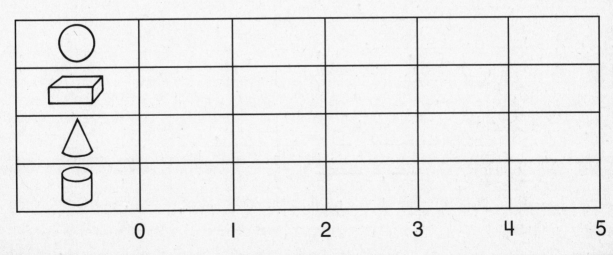

Plane Figures and Solids

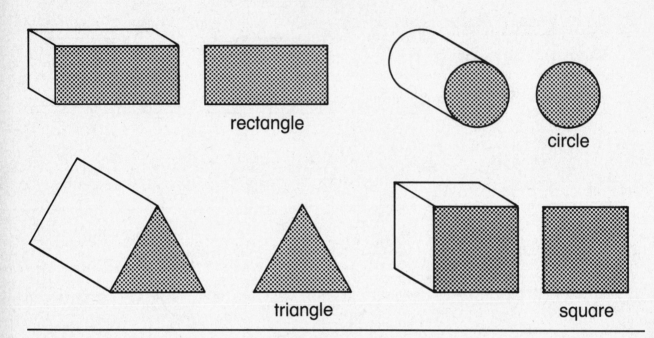

rectangle

circle

triangle

square

Color the flat face that matches the solid.

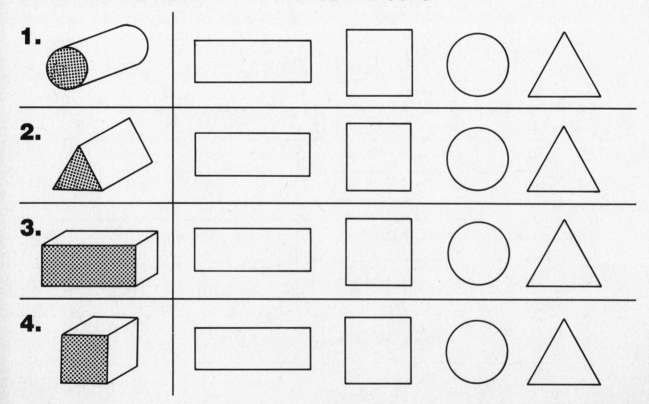

Name _____

Sides and Corners

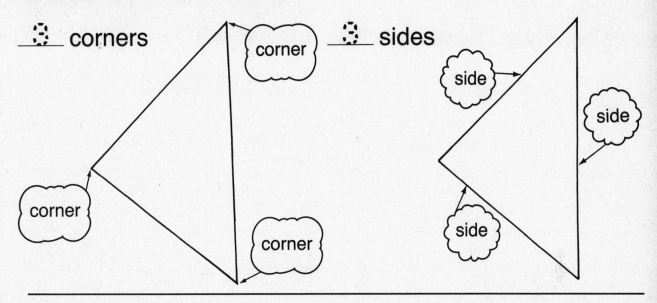

__3__ corners

__3__ sides

Where is the bug sitting? Ring the answer.
Tell how many sides and corners there are.

1.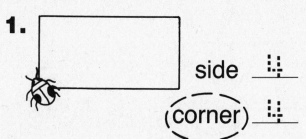

side ___4___

(corner) ___4___

2.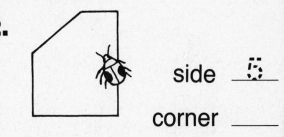

side ___5___

corner ___

3.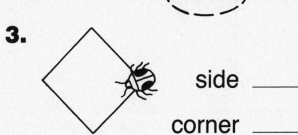

side ___

corner ___

4.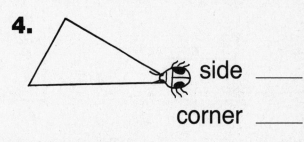

side ___

corner ___

5.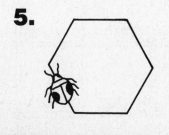

side ___

corner ___

6.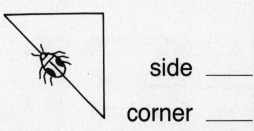

side ___

corner ___

My Geometry Book

Match the words and shapes.

circle

triangle

square

rectangle

Understanding the Operations

Read the story.
Use punchout coins to solve.
Color the coins to answer the question.

1. Luis has 3¢. 	He wants to buy 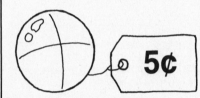 5¢	How much more does he need? 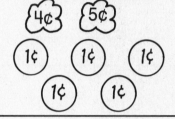
2. Kate has 5¢.	She wants to buy  8¢	How much more does she need? 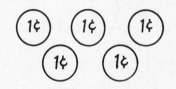
3. Josh has 6¢. 	Hee wants to buy  11¢	How much more does he need? 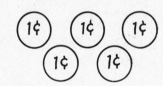

Inside, Outside, and On

Write how many pegs.

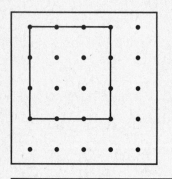

inside

outside

on

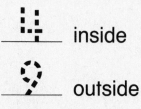

___ inside

___ outside

___ on

Make the figure on your geoboard.
Write how many pegs inside, outside, and on.

1.

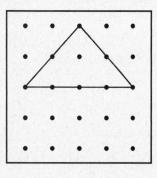

___ inside

___ outside

___ on

2.

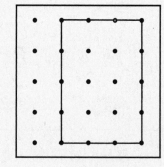

___ inside

___ outside

___ on

3.

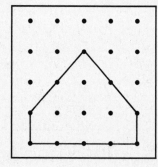

___ inside

___ outside

___ on

Symmetric Figures

Use a ruler. Draw a line from dot to dot.
Now see the matching parts.

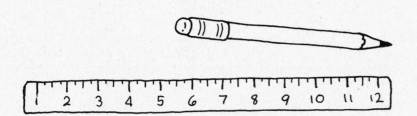

line of
symmetry

1.

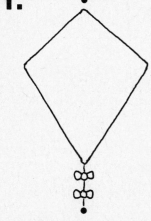

2. Draw a line to make two matching parts.

Congruent Figures

Match the figures that have the same size and shape.
Color matching figures the same color.

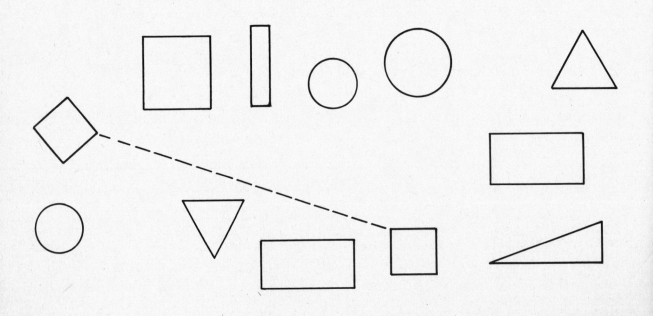

Name _____

Finding Data from a Map

Use your inch ruler to solve.
Write how many inches.

1. Andy Ant went from

 to  .

How far did he go?

2 inches +
2 inches   _____ inches

First, find the path from home to school.
Then measure each part of the path.
Add the 2 measures.

2. Betty Beetle went from

 to the 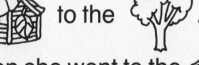 .

Then she went to the 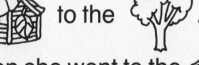 .

How far did she go?

_____ inches

How far is Betty Beetle

from now?

_____ inches

Name _____

Subtracting from 9 and 10

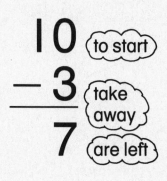

$$10 \text{ (to start)}$$
$$-3 \text{ (take away)}$$
$$7 \text{ (are left)}$$

Subtract. Use your and counters to help.

1.
$$\begin{array}{r} 10 \\ -\ 7 \\ \hline 3 \end{array}$$
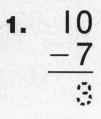
$$\begin{array}{r} 9 \\ -\ 4 \\ \hline \end{array}$$
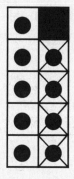
$$\begin{array}{r} 9 \\ -\ 3 \\ \hline \end{array}$$
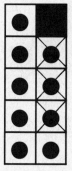

2.
$$\begin{array}{r} 10 \\ -\ 4 \\ \hline \end{array}$$
$$\begin{array}{r} 10 \\ -\ 6 \\ \hline \end{array}$$
$$\begin{array}{r} 9 \\ -\ 5 \\ \hline \end{array}$$
$$\begin{array}{r} 9 \\ -\ 6 \\ \hline \end{array}$$
$$\begin{array}{r} 10 \\ -\ 2 \\ \hline \end{array}$$

3.
$$\begin{array}{r} 9 \\ -\ 2 \\ \hline \end{array}$$
$$\begin{array}{r} 10 \\ -\ 5 \\ \hline \end{array}$$
$$\begin{array}{r} 9 \\ -\ 7 \\ \hline \end{array}$$
$$\begin{array}{r} 10 \\ -\ 8 \\ \hline \end{array}$$
$$\begin{array}{r} 10 \\ -\ 3 \\ \hline \end{array}$$

Name _____

Fact Practice

Subtract.

11 −2 9	8 −1 7	4 −4 0	3 −0 3	10 −6 4	10 −8 2

count-back facts   zero facts   10-frame facts

---

1. count-back facts

9 −2	7 −1	10 −3	6 −1	8 −3

2. zero facts

8 −8	5 −0	7 −0	6 −6	9 −0

3. 10-frame facts

10 −5	9 −4	10 −7	9 −5	10 −9

4.

7 −7	10 −8	9 −1	6 −0	10 −6	12 −3

Name _____

Understanding the Operations

Write the addition or subtraction sentence
for each story.

1. 4 rabbits are sleeping.
3 rabbits are hopping.
How many rabbits are
there in all?

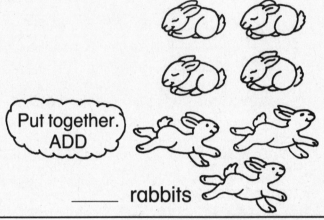

Put together.
ADD

4 ◯ 3 = _____   _____ rabbits

2. 5 dogs were sitting.
3 dogs ran away.
How many are still
sitting?

Take away.
SUBTRACT

_____ ◯ _____ = _____   _____ dogs

3. 5 snails are walking.
2 snails are jogging.
How many more
snails are walking?

Compare.
SUBTRACT

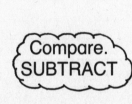

_____ ◯ _____ = _____   _____ more snails

Counting Up to Subtract

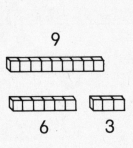

$$\begin{array}{r} 9 \\ -6 \\ \hline 3 \end{array}$$

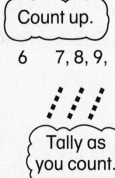

Count up.

6   7, 8, 9,

Count up
3 numbers.

Tally as
you count.

Count up to subtract.
Tally as you count.

1. $\begin{array}{r} 7 \\ -5 \\ \hline 2 \end{array}$ ⟨5, 6, 7⟩   **2.** $\begin{array}{r} 9 \\ -8 \\ \hline \end{array}$ ⟨8   9⟩   **3.** $\begin{array}{r} 10 \\ -7 \\ \hline \end{array}$ ⟨7   8, 9, 10⟩

4. $\begin{array}{r} 8 \\ -6 \\ \hline \end{array}$ ⟨6   7, 8⟩   **5.** $\begin{array}{r} 10 \\ -9 \\ \hline \end{array}$ ⟨9   10⟩   **6.** $\begin{array}{r} 8 \\ -5 \\ \hline \end{array}$ ⟨5   6, 7, 8⟩

Ring the count-up facts.
Then subtract all.

7. $\begin{array}{r} 6 \\ -5 \\ \hline \end{array}$ **8.** $\begin{array}{r} 8 \\ -2 \\ \hline \end{array}$ **9.** $\begin{array}{r} 10 \\ -8 \\ \hline \end{array}$ **10.** $\begin{array}{r} 9 \\ -7 \\ \hline \end{array}$

11. $\begin{array}{r} 11 \\ -9 \\ \hline \end{array}$ **12.** $\begin{array}{r} 12 \\ -3 \\ \hline \end{array}$ **13.** $\begin{array}{r} 9 \\ -9 \\ \hline \end{array}$ **14.** $\begin{array}{r} 5 \\ -4 \\ \hline \end{array}$

Fact Practice

Subtract.

10	12	9	10	8	11
− 2	− 3	− 4	− 6	− 5	− 9
6	9	5	4	3	2

count-back facts   10-frame facts   count-up facts

---

1. count-back facts

	7	9	10	11	8
	− 2	− 1	− 3	− 2	− 3

2. 10-frame facts

	10	9	10	10	10
	− 7	− 5	− 6	− 8	− 9

3. count-up facts

	9	8	11	9	12
	− 7	− 5	− 9	− 6	− 9

4.

10	7	8	9	10	9
− 5	− 1	− 6	− 8	− 2	− 4

Adding to Check Subtraction

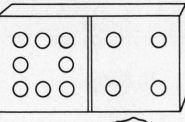

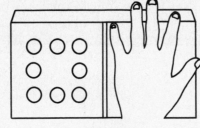

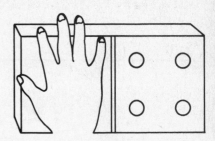

$$\begin{array}{r} 8 \\ +\,4 \\ \hline 12 \end{array}$$

$$\begin{array}{r} 12 \\ -\,4 \\ \hline 8 \end{array}$$

$$\begin{array}{r} 12 \\ -\,8 \\ \hline 4 \end{array}$$

Finish the add-to-check fact. Then subtract.

1.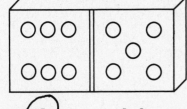

$$\begin{array}{r} 6 \\ +\,5 \\ \hline \end{array} \qquad \begin{array}{r} 11 \\ -\,5 \\ \hline \end{array} \qquad \begin{array}{r} 11 \\ -\,6 \\ \hline \end{array}$$

2.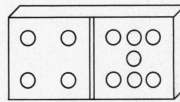

$$\begin{array}{r} 4 \\ +\,7 \\ \hline \end{array} \qquad \begin{array}{r} 11 \\ -\,7 \\ \hline \end{array} \qquad \begin{array}{r} 11 \\ -\,4 \\ \hline \end{array}$$

3.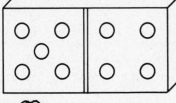

$$\begin{array}{r} 5 \\ +\,4 \\ \hline \end{array} \qquad \begin{array}{r} 9 \\ -\,4 \\ \hline \end{array} \qquad \begin{array}{r} 9 \\ -\,5 \\ \hline \end{array}$$

4.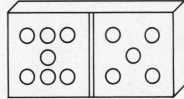

$$\begin{array}{r} 7 \\ +\,5 \\ \hline \end{array} \qquad \begin{array}{r} 12 \\ -\,5 \\ \hline \end{array} \qquad \begin{array}{r} 12 \\ -\,7 \\ \hline \end{array}$$

Fact Families

4 + 7 = 11

| 4 |
| 7 |
| 11 |

11 − 4 = 7

7 + 4 = 11

11 − 7 = 4

Add or subtract. Use counters.

1. 8 + 4 = ___   12 − 8 = ___

4 + 8 = ___   12 − 4 = ___

Make a fact family. Add or subtract.

2.

5 + 6 = ___

6 + 5 = ___

11 − 5 = ___

11 − 6 = ___

3.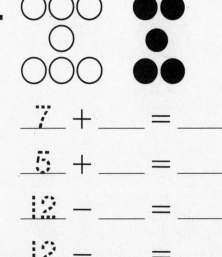

7 + ___ = ___

5 + ___ = ___

12 − ___ = ___

12 − ___ = ___

Name _____

Fact Practice

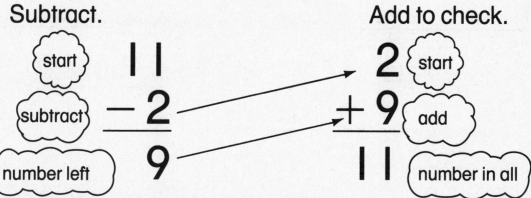

Subtract.

start — 11
subtract — − 2
number left — 9

Add to check.

2 — start
+ 9 — add
11 — number in all

Subtract. Finish the add-to-check fact.

1.
$$\begin{array}{r} 12 \\ -9 \\ \hline 3 \end{array} \qquad \begin{array}{r} 9 \\ +3 \\ \hline 12 \end{array}$$

$$\begin{array}{r} 10 \\ -4 \\ \hline \end{array} \qquad \begin{array}{r} 4 \\ + \\ \hline \end{array}$$

2.
$$\begin{array}{r} 11 \\ -3 \\ \hline \end{array} \qquad \begin{array}{r} 3 \\ + \\ \hline \end{array}$$

$$\begin{array}{r} 9 \\ -4 \\ \hline \end{array} \qquad \begin{array}{r} 4 \\ + \\ \hline \end{array}$$

3.
$$\begin{array}{r} 10 \\ -7 \\ \hline \end{array} \qquad \begin{array}{r} 7 \\ + \\ \hline \end{array}$$

$$\begin{array}{r} 9 \\ -6 \\ \hline \end{array} \qquad \begin{array}{r} 6 \\ + \\ \hline \end{array}$$

4.
$$\begin{array}{r} 11 \\ -5 \\ \hline \end{array} \qquad \begin{array}{r} 5 \\ + \\ \hline \end{array}$$

$$\begin{array}{r} 12 \\ -8 \\ \hline \end{array} \qquad \begin{array}{r} 8 \\ + \\ \hline \end{array}$$

Name _____

Telling a Story

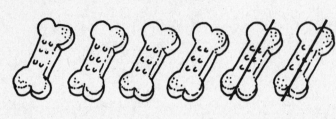

Cross out 2.

$$\underline{6} \bigodot \underline{2} = \underline{4}$$

<u>6</u> dog treats   <u>2</u> were eaten.   <u>4</u> dog treats are left.

Tell a story.
Finish the number sentence.

1.

Cross out some. $\underline{5} \bigodot \underline{} = \underline{}$

<u>5</u> cats   _____ went away.

_____ cats are left.

2.

Add the groups. $\underline{} \bigoplus \underline{} = \underline{}$

_____ gerbils   _____ fish

_____ pets in all.

3.

Cross out some. $\underline{} \bigcirc \underline{} = \underline{}$

_____ birds   _____ flew away.

_____ birds are left.

Grouping by Tens

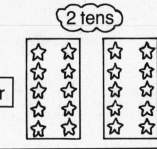

Tens	Ones
2	4

Ring groups of ten.

Write how many tens and how many extra ones.

1.

Tens	Ones
2	3

2.

Tens	Ones

3.

Tens	Ones

4.

Tens	Ones

Showing Tens and Ones

Tens	Ones
2	3

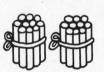 2 tens 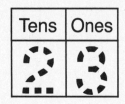   3 ones

---

Ring the tens and ones.

1.

Tens	Ones
3	4

 3 tens   4 ones

2.

Tens	Ones
2	5

 2 tens   Ring 5 ones.

3.

Tens	Ones
1	7

4.

Tens	Ones
2	8

5.

Tens	Ones
3	0

Decade Numbers and Names

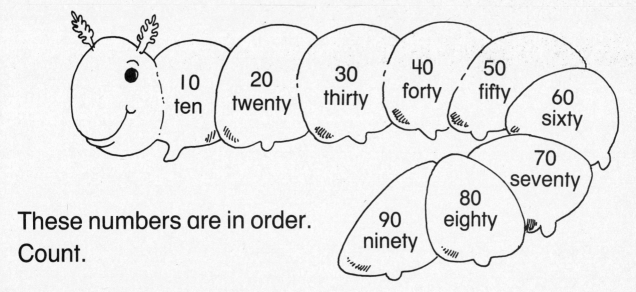

These numbers are in order.
Count.

See the caterpillar change.
Connect the dots in order. Start with 10.

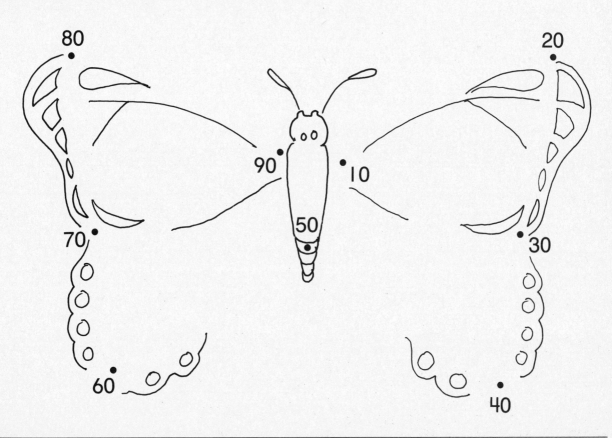

Showing and Writing 2-Digit Numbers

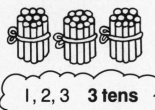 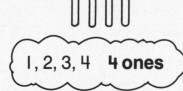 

1, 2, 3   **3 tens**   1, 2, 3, 4   **4 ones**

Count the tens and ones.
Write the number.

1.

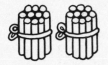

1, 2   **2 tens**   l   **l one**

2.

1, 2, 3   **3 tens**   1, 2, 3, 4, 5   **5 ones**

3.

4.

5.

6.

Name _____

Counting Tens and Ones

Follow the ↓ . Write how many.

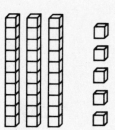

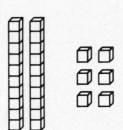

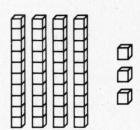

Tens	Ones
3	5

↓ ↓

| 3 5 |

Tens	Ones

↓ ↓

Tens	Ones

↓ ↓

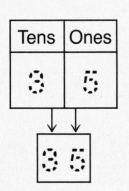

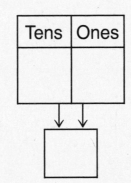

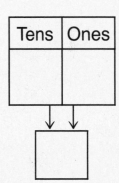

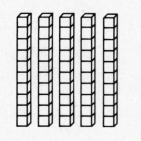

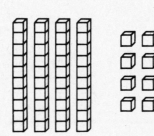

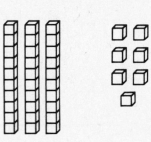

Tens	Ones

↓ ↓

Tens	Ones

↓ ↓

Tens	Ones

↓ ↓

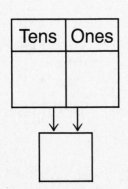

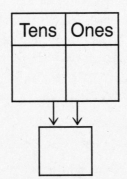

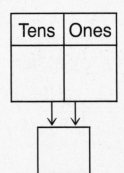

Name _____

Understanding the Operations

Ten in a box.
Each box
is I ten.

2 tens   +   2 tens = 4 tens

There are 4 tens in all.

Read the question.
Finish the number sentence.

1. How many ⟨▭⟩ and ⟨▭⟩ in all?

3 tens ◯ 4 tens = _____ tens

2. How many more ⟨▭⟩ than ⟨▭⟩ are there?

5 tens ◯ 2 tens = _____ tens

Trading Dimes and Pennies

10 pennies —— is the same as ——→ 1 dime.

Use your penny and dime punchouts.
Show with pennies. Trade for dimes.
Ring the correct amount.

1.

21 pennies

2.

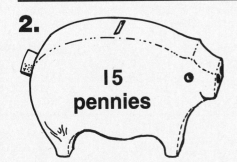

15 pennies

3.

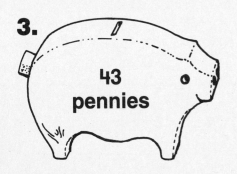

43 pennies

Dimes and Pennies

Count the money. Write the amount.

1.

10   20   30   31   31 ¢

2.

10   20   21   ___   ___   ___   ___   ___ ¢

3.

10   ___   ___   ___   ___ ¢

4.

10   ___   ___   ___   ___ ¢

Making Estimates

Stickers come in strips of ten.

 10 stickers

---

Without counting, tell about how many.
Ring your estimate. Ring tens to check.

1.

About how many stickers?

10   30   40   70

2.

About how many stickers?

20   50   70   90

3.

About how many stickers?

20   40   60   80

4.

About how many stickers?

10   20   30   40

Name _____

Counting to 50

 I see a pattern!

1	2	3	4	5	6	7	8	9	10
11	12	13	14	15	16	17	18	19	20
21	22	23	24	25	26	27	28	29	30
31	32	33	34	35	36	37	38	39	40
41	42	43	44	45	46	47	48	49	50

Count. Write how many.

1.

22

23   2   2   2   2

2.

39

40   ___   ___   ___   ___

3.

CRAYONS

16

___   ___   ___   ___   ___

Counting to 100

Write the number that is one more.

1.

39 and 1 more is 40.

2.
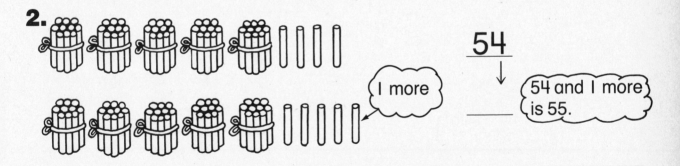

54 and 1 more is 55.

3.

41 and 1 more is 48.

Counting On and Back

Count back 1 each time.

Count on 1 each time.

Tens	Ones
3	6

3͟4͟ ← 3͟5͟ ← | 3 | 6 | → 3͟7͟ → 3͟8͟

Count on and back.
Write the numbers.

Count back.   ← | Tens | Ones | →   Count on.

1. 5 ___   5 ___ | 5 | 5 | 5 ___   5 ___

Count back.   ← | Tens | Ones | →   Count on.

2. 4 ___   4 ___ | 4 | 4 | 4 ___   4 ___

Count back.   ← | Tens | Ones | →   Count on.

3. ___ ___   ___ ___ | 7 | 1 | ___ ___   ___ ___

---

4. Check by counting.
Start with the smallest number in each row.

Numbers Before, After, and Between

15	16	17
before 16 1 less than 16	between 15 and 17	after 16 1 more than 16

Write the number that comes before.

1 less	1 less	1 less

1. 37 | | 56 | | | 82 |

| | 72 | | 41 | | | 99 |

Write the number that comes after.

1 more

2. | 67 | | | 91 | | | 65 | |

| 29 | | | 51 | | | 19 | |

Write the number that comes between.

3. | 23 | 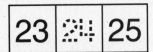 | 25 | | 96 | | 98 |

| 45 | | 47 | | 59 | | 61 |

Name _____

Comparing Numbers

4 ones are more than 2 ones.

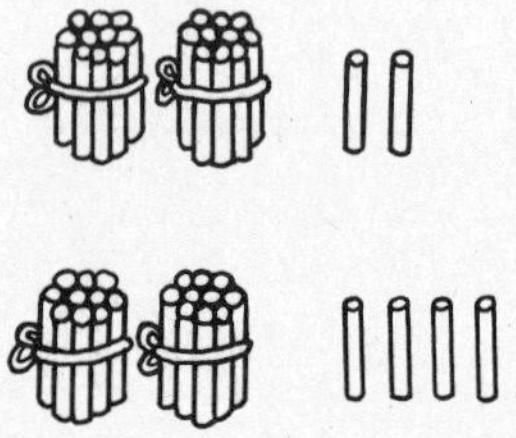

22

(24)

3 tens are more than 2 tens.

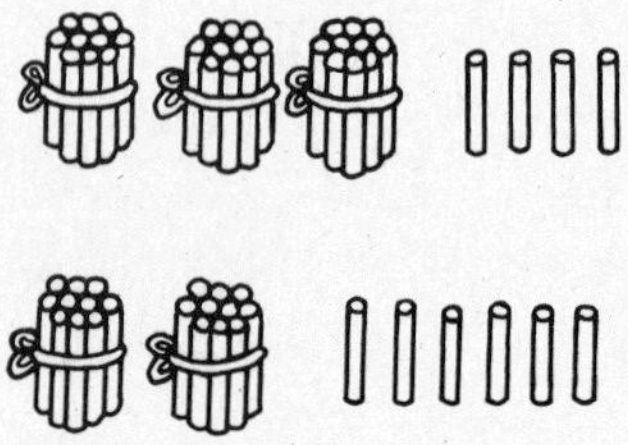

(34)

26

Ring the number that shows more.

1.

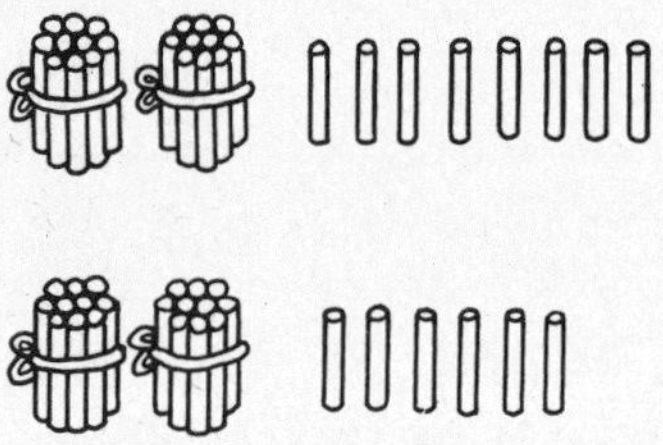

28

26

2.

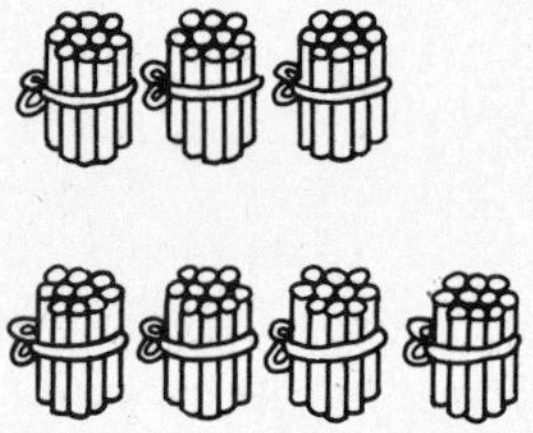

30

40

3.

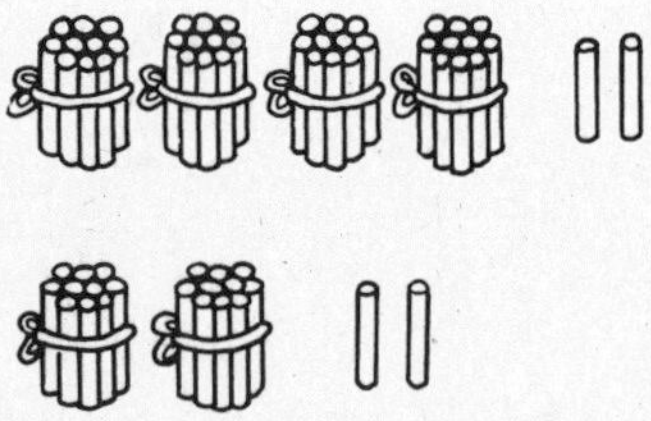

42

22

4.

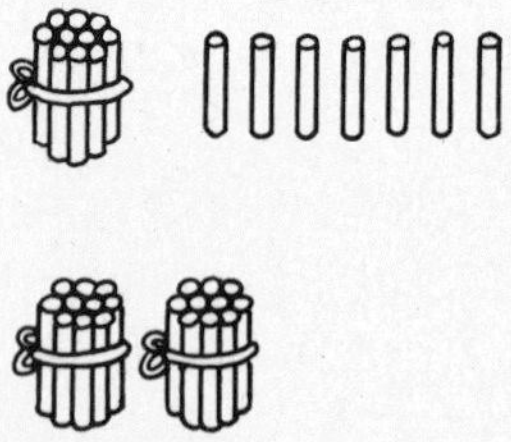

17

20

5.

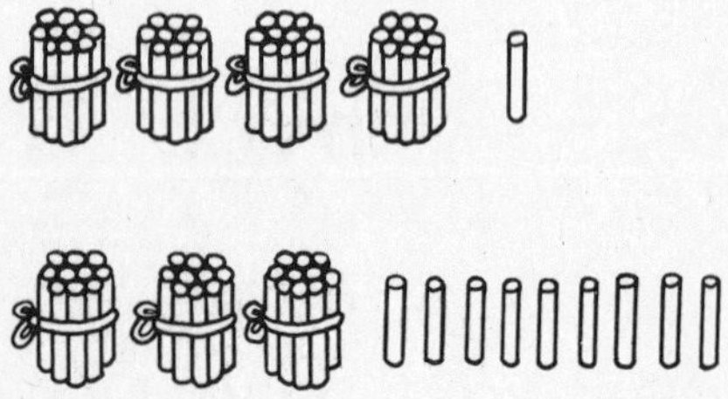

41

39

6.

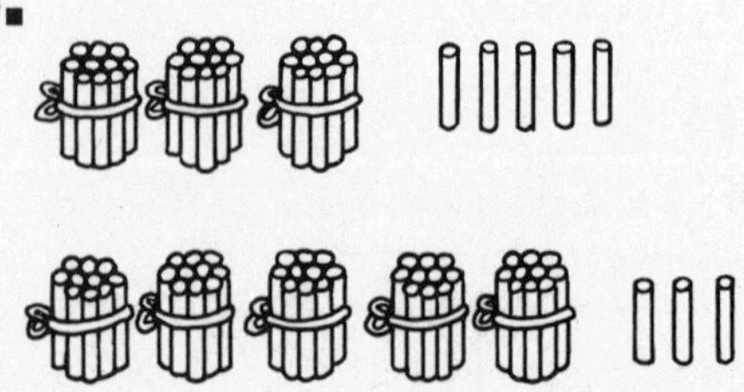

35

53

Use with text pages 255–256.

RS-1

Name _____

Understanding the Operations

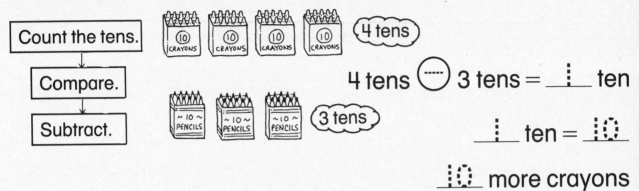

Count the tens.	4 tens

4 tens $\ominus$ 3 tens = __1__ ten

| Compare. |
| Subtract. |

3 tens

__1__ ten = __10__

__10__ more crayons

---

1. How many more crayons than pencils are there?

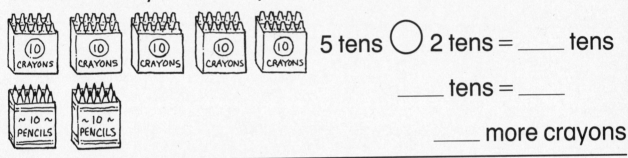

5 tens $\bigcirc$ 2 tens = _____ tens

_____ tens = _____

_____ more crayons

---

2. How many more crayons than pencils are there?

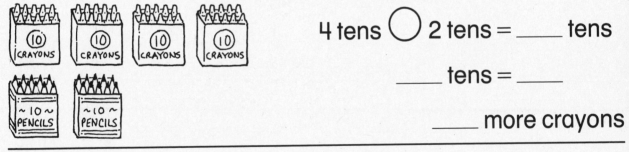

4 tens $\bigcirc$ 2 tens = _____ tens

_____ tens = _____

_____ more crayons

---

3. How many more pencils than crayons are there?

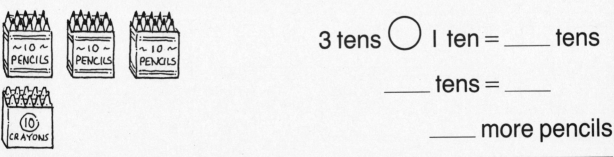

3 tens $\bigcirc$ 1 ten = _____ tens

_____ tens = _____

_____ more pencils

RS-1 **107**

Name _____

Counting Patterns for 10s

Use your hundreds chart to help you count.
Start at the top of the ladder
Write the number that is ten more.

I more ten

32
42
52

The ones stay the same.

Start at the top of the ladder.
Write each time you count ten more.

1.

10
20
30
40

2.

45
55

3.

37
47

4.

23
33

5.

25
35

6.

34
44

7.

19
29

8.

60
70

Counting Patterns for 2s and 5s

Count by twos. Write how many.

2	4	6	8	10	12	14	16	18	20

2 more   2 more

Count by fives. Write how many.

5	10	15	20	25	30	35	40	45	50

5 more   5 more

1. Count by twos. Write how many.

2	4								

2. Count by fives. Write how many.

5	10								

Name _____

Ordinal Numbers

1st	2nd	3rd	4th	5th	6th	7th	8th	9th	10th
first	second	third	fourth	fifth	sixth	seventh	eighth	ninth	tenth

Ring where the tall one is in line.

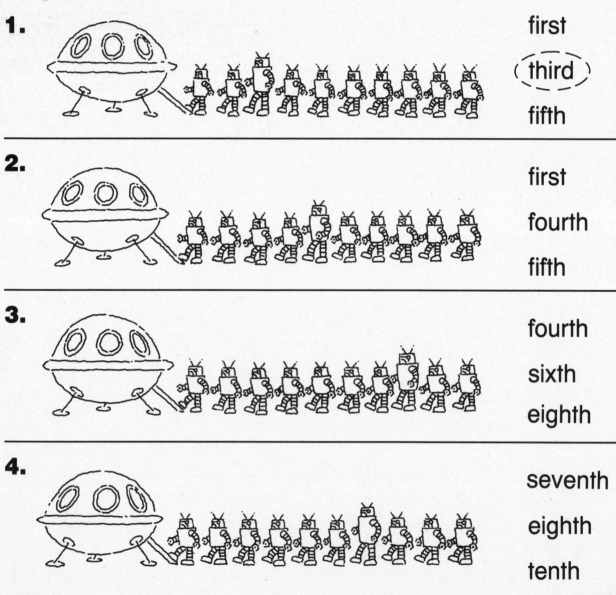

1.
first
(third)
fifth

2.
first
fourth
fifth

3.
fourth
sixth
eighth

4.
seventh
eighth
tenth

Name _____

Finding Extra Data

Pedro had 8 toy cars.
He gave 2 toy cars to his little brother.

He gave 2 toy cars to his little brother.
His brother is 5 years old.

You do not need to know how old Pedro's brother is.

How many toy cars does Pedro have now?

$8 \ominus 2 = 6$ He has __6__ toy cars.

Read the story. Look for the data you need to answer the
question. Write the number sentence and the answer.
Draw a line under the extra data.

1. Ellen has 6 dolls.
Jill has 4 dolls. 2 of Jill's dolls have long hair.
How many more dolls does Ellen have?

$6 \ominus 4 = $ ____   Ellen has ____ more dolls.

---

2. Su Lee made 7 bracelets.
She made 3 necklaces. Then she made 2 more bracelets.
How many bracelets did Su Lee make in all?

____ ◯ ____ = ____   She made ____ bracelets.

---

3. Howie has 10 bugs in a jar.
3 are ladybugs. He lets 4 bugs out of the jar.
How many bugs does Howie have now?

____ ◯ ____ = ____   He has ____ bugs.

Name _____

Counting Dimes and Pennies

I dime = 10¢

is like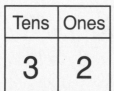

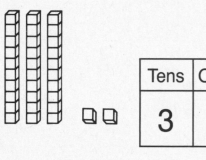

Tens	Ones
3	2

32

 is like

32¢

Dimes	Pennies
3	2

Write the number of dimes and pennies. Write the price.

1.

Dimes	Pennies
2	3

 ¢

2.

Dimes	Pennies
1	5

○ ¢

3.

Dimes	Pennies
4	1

 ¢

4.

Dimes	Pennies
3	4

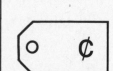 ¢

Counting Nickels and Pennies

__5__ , __10__ , __11__ , __12__ , __13__

Count the money. Write the price.

1.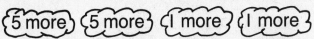

¢

_____ , _____ , _____ , _____ ,

2.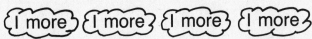

¢

_____ , _____ , _____ , _____ ,

3.

¢

_____ , _____ , _____ , _____ ,

Name _____

Counting Dimes and Nickels

Count dimes by tens.
Count nickels by fives. Write the price.

1.

<u>10</u> , <u>20</u> , <u>30</u> , <u>35</u> , <u>40</u>

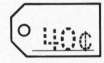

2.

____ , ____ , ____ , ____ , ____

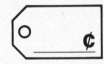¢

3.

____ , ____ , ____ , ____ , ____

¢

4.

____ , ____ , ____ , ____ , ____

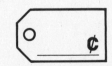¢

Use with text pages 275 – 276.

Name _____

Counting Dimes, Nickels, and Pennies

10¢   10¢   5¢   1¢   1¢   1¢

_10_ , _20_ , _25_ , _26_ , _27_ , _28_   ⃝ 28¢

10 more   5 more   1 more   1 more   1 more

Count the money. Write the price.

1.

_10_ , ____ , ____ , ____   ⃝ ___¢

5 more   5 more   1 more

2.

_10_ , ____ , ____ , ____ , ____   ⃝ ___¢

10 more   5 more   5 more   5 more

3.

____ , ____ , ____ , ____ , ____ , ____   ⃝ ___¢

Name _____

Counting and Comparing Money

Count the money. Write the prices.
Ring the one that is less.

1.

<u>10</u> , <u>20</u> , <u>25</u> , <u>30</u> , <u>31</u>

<u>10</u> , <u>15</u> , <u>20</u> , <u>21</u> , <u>22</u>

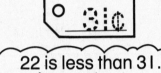

31¢

22 is less than 31.

22¢

2.

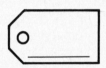

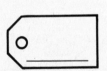

3.

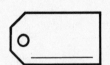

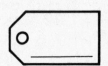

Name _____

Understanding the Operations

Draw more or cross out some to help solve.
Then add or subtract. Finish the sentence.

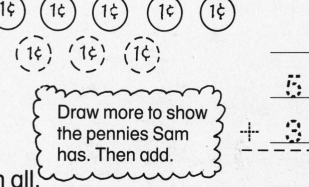

1. Nan has 5 pennies.
Sam has 3 pennies.
How many pennies
are there in all?

Draw more to show
the pennies Sam
has. Then add.

$\begin{array}{r} 5 \\ +\ 3 \\ \hline \end{array}$

There are ____ pennies in all.

---

2. José had 6 dimes.
He spent 2 dimes.
How many dimes does
he have left?

Cross out to show
the dimes José spent.
Then subtract.

José has ____ dimes left.

---

3. Linda had 4 dimes.
She got 5 more dimes.
How many dimes does
Linda have now?

Linda has ____ dimes.

Name _____

Counting Quarters and Other Coins

Use 1 , 3 , 2   , and 2 punchouts.

Cover each coin as you count. Match the amount.

1. 	
25 , 35 , 45 , 50 , 51	**55¢**
2. _____ , _____ , _____ , _____	**40¢**
3. _____ , _____ , _____	**51¢**
4. _____ , _____ , _____	**37¢**

Name _____

Using Data from a Newspaper Ad

| Find out how much money the child has. | → | Read the ad to find the price of what is wanted. | → | Compare the two amounts. | → | Tell whether or not there is enough money. |

  SEED SALE
25¢   29¢
10¢   16¢   37¢   18¢

1. Anya has 41¢. She wants to buy .

How much are the ? _37¢_

Does she have enough money?   (yes)   no

2. Carlos has 26¢. He wants to buy .

How much are the ? _____

Does he have enough money?   yes   no

3. Harold has 37¢. He wants to buy .

How much are the ? _____

Does he have enough money?   yes   no

Name _____

Clock Parts

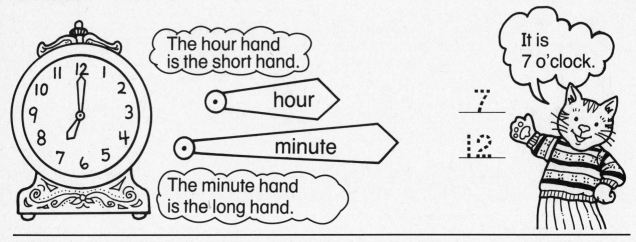

The hour hand is the short hand.

hour

minute

The minute hand is the long hand.

It is 7 o'clock.

7
12

Where are the hands? Write the numbers.

1.

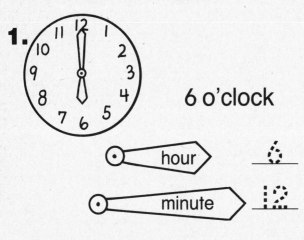

6 o'clock

hour   6

minute   12

2.

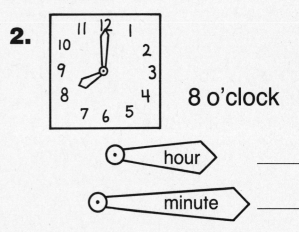

8 o'clock

hour   ____

minute   ____

3.

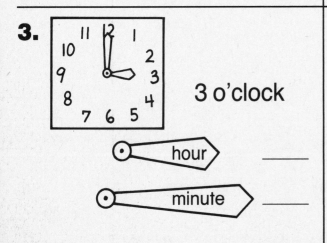

3 o'clock

hour   ____

minute   ____

4

10 o'clock

hour   ____

minute   ____

120   Use with text pages 291 – 292.   **RS-1**

Time on the Hour

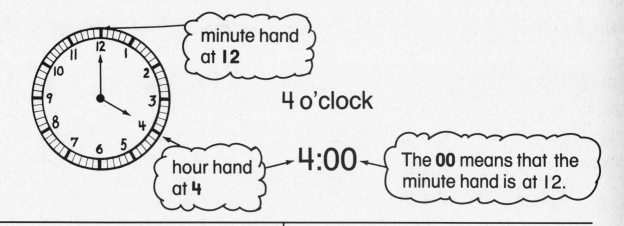

minute hand at **12**

4 o'clock

hour hand at **4**

4:00

The **00** means that the minute hand is at **12**.

Write the time.

1.

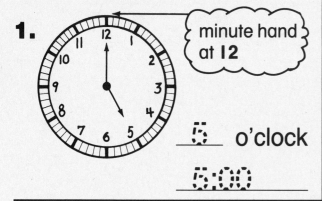

minute hand at **12**

_5_ o'clock

5:00

2.

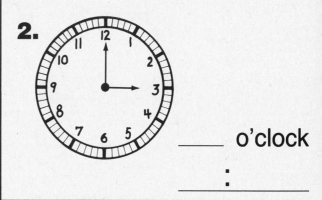

_____ o'clock

___:___

3.

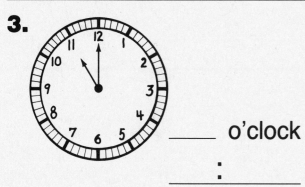

_____ o'clock

___:___

4.

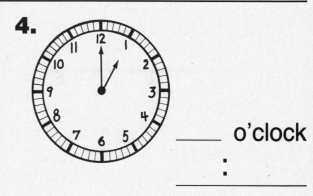

_____ o'clock

___:___

Understanding the Operations

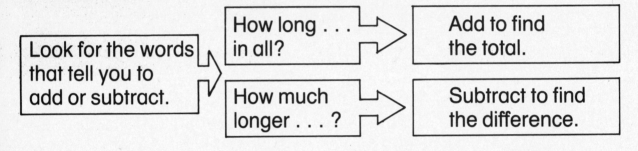

Add or subtract to answer the question.

1. Meg read a book for 2 hours.
She read a magazine for
1 hour.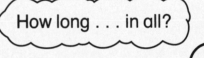

How long did Meg read in all? _____ hours

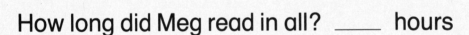

---

2. Larry did knee bends for 8 minutes.
He did sit-ups for 5 minutes.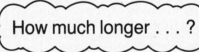

How much longer did
Larry do knee bends? _____ minutes

---

3. Tina's family went to an island.
They drove for 5 hours.
They took a boat for 2 hours.

How long was the trip in all? _____ hours

Time on the Half Hour

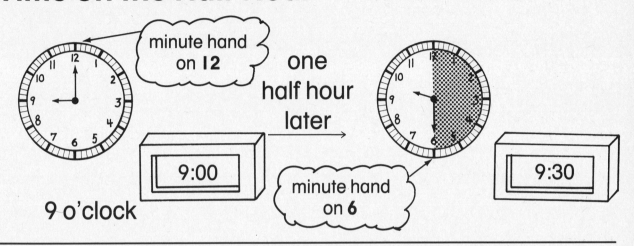

minute hand on **12**

one half hour later

9:00

9 o'clock

minute hand on **6**

9:30

Make the clocks show the time one half hour later.

1.

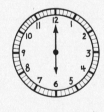

2.

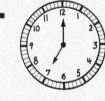

3.

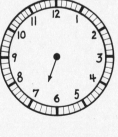

4.

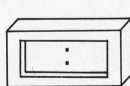

Name _____

The Mouse Family's Time Book

Draw the hands to show the time.

1.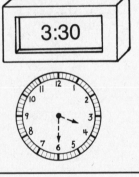

3:30

2.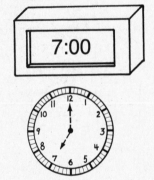

7:00

3.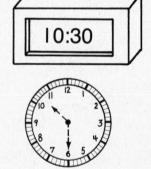

10:30

4.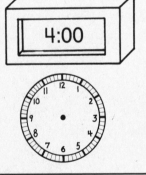

4:00

5.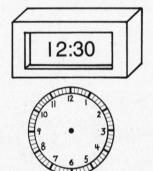

12:30

6.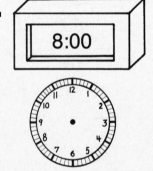

8:00

7.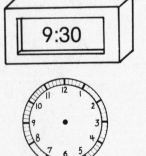

9:30

8.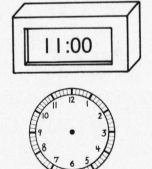

11:00

9.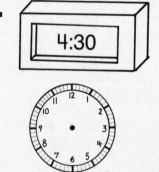

4:30

Name _____

Calendar

This month has 30 days. It begins on **Tuesday.**
Write the dates.

SEPTEMBER

Sunday	Monday	Tuesday	Wednesday	Thursday	Friday	Saturday
		1	2	3	4	5
6						

This month has 31 days. It begins on **Thursday.**
Write the dates.

OCTOBER

Sunday	Monday	Tuesday	Wednesday	Thursday	Friday	Saturday

Using Data from a Chart

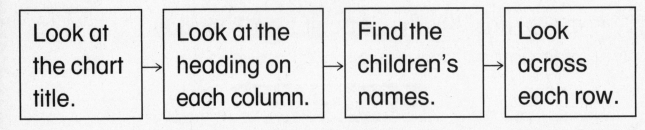

| Look at the chart title. | → | Look at the heading on each column. | → | Find the children's names. | → | Look across each row. |

Hours Spent

	In the Car	Playing in the Sand	Eating Lunch	Swimming	Tossing the Ball
Michelle	I	2	half hour	2	half hour
Mike	I	3	half hour	I	I

Ring the answer.

1. How long did Mike play in the sand? I hour   2 hours   (3 hours)

2. How long did Michelle swim? half hour   2 hours   3 hours

3. How much time did each spend in the car? I hour   2 hours   I hour

4. What else did they spend the same time at? playing in the sand   eating lunch   tossing the ball

Adding 9

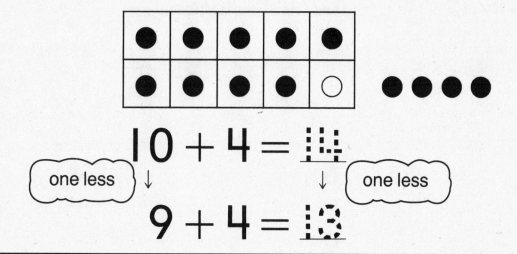

$$10 + 4 = 14$$

one less ↓   ↓ one less

$$9 + 4 = 13$$

Add.

1.
$$\begin{array}{r} 9 \\ +5 \\ \hline 14 \end{array}$$
(10 + 5 = 15
I less is ?)

$$\begin{array}{r} 9 \\ +8 \\ \hline \end{array}$$
(10 + 8 = 18
I less is ?)

2.
$$\begin{array}{r} 9 \\ +6 \\ \hline \end{array}$$
$$\begin{array}{r} 9 \\ +9 \\ \hline \end{array}$$
$$\begin{array}{r} 9 \\ +7 \\ \hline \end{array}$$
$$\begin{array}{r} 2 \\ +9 \\ \hline \end{array}$$
$$\begin{array}{r} 9 \\ +3 \\ \hline \end{array}$$

3.
$$\begin{array}{r} 8 \\ +9 \\ \hline \end{array}$$
$$\begin{array}{r} 9 \\ +4 \\ \hline \end{array}$$
$$\begin{array}{r} 3 \\ +9 \\ \hline \end{array}$$
$$\begin{array}{r} 5 \\ +9 \\ \hline \end{array}$$
$$\begin{array}{r} 6 \\ +9 \\ \hline \end{array}$$

4. $7 + 9 =$ ___ $9 + 8 =$ ___ $5 + 9 =$ ___

Name _____

Doubles Through 9 + 9

Match the picture and the double fact.
Write the sum.

6 eggs in each row.

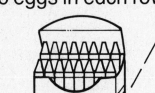

8 crayons in each row.

$8 + 8 =$ ____

$6 + 6 =$ ____

$9 + 9 =$ ____

$7 + 7 =$ ____

7 days in each week.

9 dots on each side.

Ring the double facts. Then add all.

1.
$$\begin{array}{r} 5 \\ +3 \\ \hline \end{array} \qquad \begin{array}{r} 4 \\ +4 \\ \hline \end{array} \qquad \begin{array}{r} 6 \\ +6 \\ \hline \end{array} \qquad \begin{array}{r} 8 \\ +8 \\ \hline \end{array} \qquad \begin{array}{r} 2 \\ +2 \\ \hline \end{array} \qquad \begin{array}{r} 9 \\ +9 \\ \hline \end{array}$$

2.
$$\begin{array}{r} 7 \\ +7 \\ \hline \end{array} \qquad \begin{array}{r} 9 \\ +3 \\ \hline \end{array} \qquad \begin{array}{r} 3 \\ +3 \\ \hline \end{array} \qquad \begin{array}{r} 4 \\ +3 \\ \hline \end{array} \qquad \begin{array}{r} 5 \\ +5 \\ \hline \end{array} \qquad \begin{array}{r} 5 \\ +6 \\ \hline \end{array}$$

Name _____

Fact Practice

Show with counters.
Draw the counters.
Add. Ring the double facts.

---

1. $6 + 6 = 12$

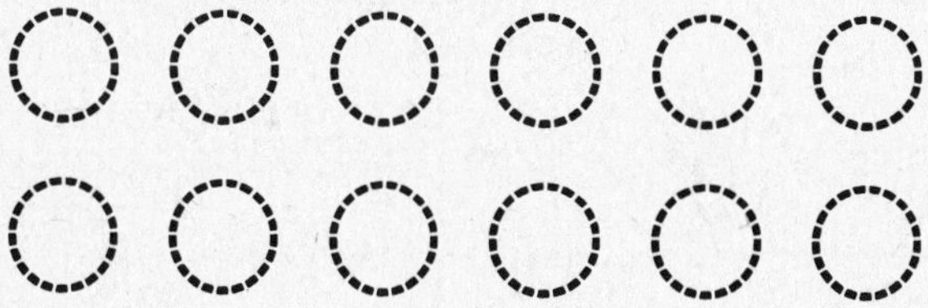

◯ ◯ ◯ ◯ ◯ ◯
◯ ◯ ◯ ◯ ◯ ◯

2. $9 + 3 = \underline{\quad}$

---

3. $8 + 8 = \underline{\quad}$

4. $9 + 9 = \underline{\quad}$

---

5. $9 + 5 = \underline{\quad}$

6. $7 + 7 = \underline{\quad}$

Name _____

Adding Three Numbers

Look for sums of 10 or doubles.
Ring the two numbers. Add.

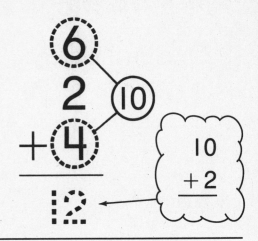

1.

3		
(5)	(8)	(7)
+(5)	(2)	1
	+ 4	+(7)

2.

4	4	4	9	1
6	3	3	2	8
+2	+4	+7	+1	+8

3.

1	2	6	3	4
9	5	3	9	7
+5	+5	+4	+3	+3

Use with text pages 315–316.

Name _____

Understanding the Operations

Use counters to show the story.
Write how many more are needed.

1.

 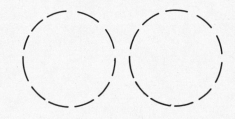

Need
5 apples.

_____ more are needed.

Apple Pie

2.

Need
6 lemons.

_____ more are needed.

Lemonade

3.

Need
8 potatoes.

Potato Soup   _____ more are needed.

Double Plus One Through 8 + 9

Match the double plus-one facts.
Find the sum. Use the double to help.

| $6 + 6 = 12$ | $8 + 8 = 16$ | $7 + 7 = 14$ |

| $7 + 8 = \underline{\quad}$ | $6 + 7 = 13$ | $8 + 9 = \underline{\quad}$ |

I more than
6 + 6

Add. (double) (double plus one)

1.
$$\begin{array}{r} 4 \\ +4 \\ \hline \end{array} \qquad \begin{array}{r} 4 \\ +5 \\ \hline \end{array} \qquad \begin{array}{r} 6 \\ +6 \\ \hline \end{array} \qquad \begin{array}{r} 6 \\ +7 \\ \hline \end{array} \qquad \begin{array}{r} 8 \\ +8 \\ \hline \end{array} \qquad \begin{array}{r} 8 \\ +9 \\ \hline \end{array}$$

2.
$$\begin{array}{r} 3 \\ +3 \\ \hline \end{array} \qquad \begin{array}{r} 4 \\ +3 \\ \hline \end{array} \qquad \begin{array}{r} 5 \\ +5 \\ \hline \end{array} \qquad \begin{array}{r} 6 \\ +5 \\ \hline \end{array} \qquad \begin{array}{r} 7 \\ +7 \\ \hline \end{array} \qquad \begin{array}{r} 8 \\ +7 \\ \hline \end{array}$$

3.
$$\begin{array}{r} 2 \\ +3 \\ \hline \end{array} \qquad \begin{array}{r} 5 \\ +4 \\ \hline \end{array} \qquad \begin{array}{r} 6 \\ +5 \\ \hline \end{array} \qquad \begin{array}{r} 7 \\ +8 \\ \hline \end{array} \qquad \begin{array}{r} 9 \\ +8 \\ \hline \end{array}$$

Name _____

Sums to 18

Draw ○ to show the second number.
Make 10. Add extra. Write the sum.

7
$+5$
$\overline{12}$

Start in the

7 ★'s
5 ○'s
12 in all

5
$+7$ turnaround fact
$\overline{12}$

---

1. 8
  $+6$

  6
  $+8$

2. 8
  $+5$
  $\overline{13}$

  5
  $+8$

---

3. 8
  $+4$

  4
  $+8$

4. 7
  $+4$
  $\overline{11}$

  4
  $+7$

Add with 9 or use doubles.

5. 8 $\quad$ 9 $\quad$ 5 $\quad$ 7 $\quad$ 8 $\quad$ 9
  $+8$ $\quad$ $+3$ $\quad$ $+9$ $\quad$ $+8$ $\quad$ $+9$ $\quad$ $+6$

Name _____

Fact Practice

Add 9

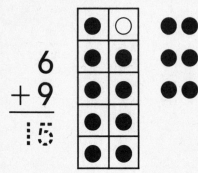

$$\begin{array}{r} 6 \\ +9 \\ \hline 15 \end{array}$$

Doubles

$$\begin{array}{r} 7 \\ +7 \\ \hline 14 \end{array}$$

Doubles Plus One

$$\begin{array}{r} 6 \to \\ +6 \to \\ \hline 12 \to \end{array} \begin{array}{r} 6 \\ +7 \\ \hline 13 \end{array}$$

1. Add 9.

$$\begin{array}{r} 4 \\ +9 \\ \hline \end{array} \qquad \begin{array}{r} 9 \\ +5 \\ \hline \end{array} \qquad \begin{array}{r} 8 \\ +9 \\ \hline \end{array} \qquad \begin{array}{r} 9 \\ +7 \\ \hline \end{array} \qquad \begin{array}{r} 9 \\ +6 \\ \hline \end{array}$$

2. Add doubles.

$$\begin{array}{r} 9 \\ +9 \\ \hline \end{array} \qquad \begin{array}{r} 5 \\ +5 \\ \hline \end{array} \qquad \begin{array}{r} 8 \\ +8 \\ \hline \end{array} \qquad \begin{array}{r} 6 \\ +6 \\ \hline \end{array} \qquad \begin{array}{r} 7 \\ +7 \\ \hline \end{array}$$

3. Add doubles plus one.

$$\begin{array}{r} 5 \\ +6 \\ \hline \end{array} \qquad \begin{array}{r} 7 \\ +8 \\ \hline \end{array} \qquad \begin{array}{r} 6 \\ +7 \\ \hline \end{array} \qquad \begin{array}{r} 8 \\ +9 \\ \hline \end{array} \qquad \begin{array}{r} 8 \\ +7 \\ \hline \end{array}$$

Determining Reasonable Answers

Write the correct number sentence.
Ring the answer if it is correct.
Cross it out if it is wrong.

1. Hans had 5 crayons.
2 were broken.
How many were not broken?

~~3~~ crayons were not broken.

> Subtract to find
> the difference.

$5 - 2 = 3$

2. Kate had 7 white marbles.
She had 4 black marbles.
How many more are white?

_3_ more marbles are white.

> Subtract to find
> how many more.

_____

3. 4 children were jumping rope.
2 more children have joined them.
How many are jumping rope now?

_2_ children are jumping rope.

> Add to find
> the total.

_____

4. 8 children are on swings.
6 children are in the sandbox.
How many more are on swings?

_14_ more children are on swings.

> Subtract to find
> how many more.

_____

Name _____

Doubles to 18

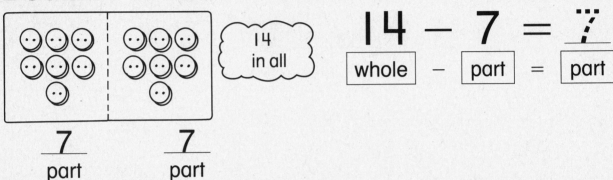

14 in all

$$14 - 7 = 7$$

whole − part = part

7 part   7 part

Write how many in each part. Subtract.

1.

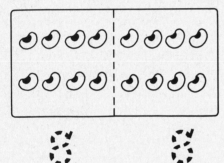

16 in all

$$16 - 8 = \underline{}$$

6   6

2.

12 in all

$$12 - 6 = \underline{}$$

___   ___

3.

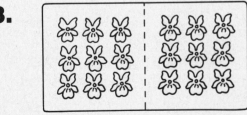

18 in all

$$18 - 9 = \underline{}$$

___   ___

Use with text pages 331 – 332.

Name _____

Subtracting 9

Cross out 9. Write what is left.

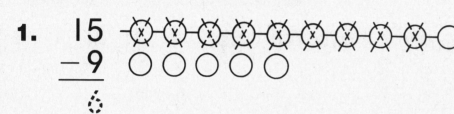

I on the string and 5 extra. 6 are left.

1. 15
-9
6

2. 13
-9

3. 16
-9

4. 14
-9

5. 17
-9

Name _____

Fact Practice

1. To subtract 1, 2, or 3, you can **count back**.

$$12 \atop -\,3 \atop \overline{\,9\,}$$ *(Begin at 12. Count back 3. 11, 10, **9**)*

$$10 \atop -\,2$$ $$11 \atop -\,3$$ $$10 \atop -\,1$$ $$11 \atop -\,2$$

---

2. When the numbers are close, you can **count up**.

$$12 \atop -\,9 \atop \overline{\,3\,}$$ *(Begin at 9. Count up to 12. 10, 11, **12** ③)*

$$10 \atop -\,9$$ $$10 \atop -\,8$$ $$9 \atop -\,7$$ $$11 \atop -\,8$$

---

3. To subtract **doubles**, think of the addition doubles.

$$14 \atop -\,7 \atop \overline{\,7\,}$$ *(7 + 7 = 14)*

$$16 \atop -\,8$$ $$10 \atop -\,5$$ $$18 \atop -\,9$$ $$12 \atop -\,6$$

---

4. To **subtract 9**, use ▦ and counters.

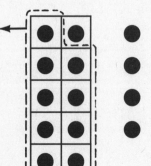 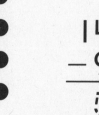

$$14 \atop -\,9 \atop \overline{\,5\,}$$ $$16 \atop -\,9$$ $$15 \atop -\,9$$ $$13 \atop -\,9$$

Understanding the Operations

6 kittens are in the basket.
4 are white. The others are black.
How many are black?

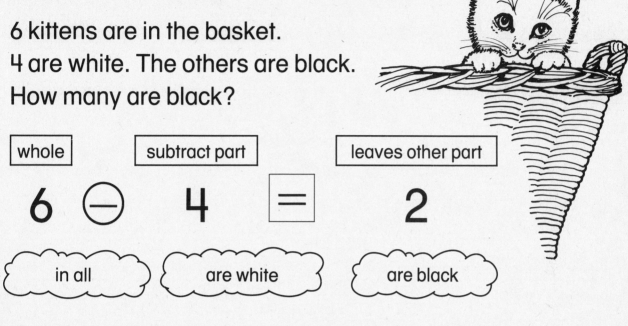

whole	subtract part	leaves other part
6 ⊖	4 ⬜=	2
in all	are white	are black

Use counters to show the story.
Finish the subtraction sentence.

1. 7 pets are in the window.
3 are kittens. The rest are
puppies. How many are
puppies?

$7 \ominus 3 = $ ___

___ puppies

---

2. 8 dogs are in the yard.
5 have spots. The others
do not have spots. How many
dogs do not have spots?

$8 \bigcirc$ ___ $=$ ___

___ dogs

Using Addition to Subtract 4, 5, and 6

Mark an X on the dots to show how many you take away.
Use the add-to-check fact and the dot card to subtract.

Take away seven.

1.

$$\begin{array}{r} 7 \\ +6 \\ \hline 13 \end{array}$$

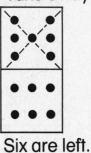

$$\begin{array}{r} 13 \\ -7 \\ \hline 6 \end{array}$$

Six are left.

2.

$$\begin{array}{r} 9 \\ +5 \\ \hline 14 \end{array}$$

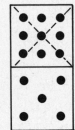

$$\begin{array}{r} 14 \\ -9 \\ \hline \end{array}$$

3.

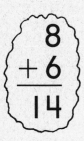

$$\begin{array}{r} 8 \\ +6 \\ \hline 14 \end{array}$$

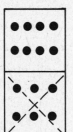

$$\begin{array}{r} 14 \\ -6 \\ \hline \end{array}$$

4.

$$\begin{array}{r} 4 \\ +9 \\ \hline 13 \end{array}$$

$$\begin{array}{r} 13 \\ -9 \\ \hline \end{array}$$

5.

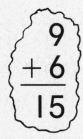

$$\begin{array}{r} 9 \\ +6 \\ \hline 15 \end{array}$$

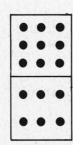

$$\begin{array}{r} 15 \\ -9 \\ \hline \end{array}$$

6.

$$\begin{array}{r} 5 \\ +8 \\ \hline 13 \end{array}$$

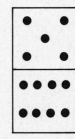

$$\begin{array}{r} 13 \\ -8 \\ \hline \end{array}$$

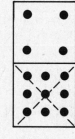

Subtract. Use the add-to-check fact.

7.

$$\begin{array}{r} 5 \\ +9 \\ \hline 14 \end{array}$$

$$\begin{array}{r} 14 \\ -5 \\ \hline \end{array}$$

8.

$$\begin{array}{r} 6 \\ +8 \\ \hline 14 \end{array}$$

$$\begin{array}{r} 14 \\ -8 \\ \hline \end{array}$$

Using Addition to Subtract 7 and 8

Shade counters red and yellow
to show the add-to-check fact.
Mark an X to show which group you
subtracted.

---

1. $5 + 8 = 13$

$13 - 8 = \underline{5}$

2. $9 + 7 = 16$

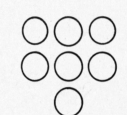

$16 - 7 = \underline{}$

---

3. $8 + 7 = 15$

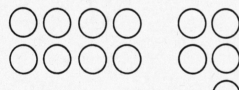

$15 - 7 = \underline{}$

4. $6 + 8 = 14$

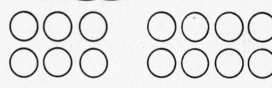

$14 - 8 = \underline{}$

---

5. $9 + 8 = 17$

$17 - 8 = \underline{}$

6. $7 + 6 = 13$

$13 - 6 = \underline{}$

Related Subtraction Facts

Write how many are in each part.
Then subtract.

1. 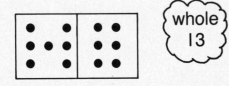 (whole 13)

(part)→ _7_ _6_ ←(part)

$13 - 6 = \underline{7}$ and

$13 - 7 = \underline{6}$

2. 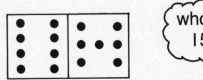 (whole 15)

part → ____ ____ ←(part)

$15 - 7 = $ ____ and

$15 - 8 = $ ____

3. 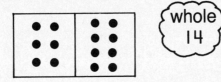 (whole 14)

(part)→ ____ ____ ←(part)

$14 - 8 = $ ____ and

$14 - 6 = $ ____

4.  (whole 16)

part → ____ ____ ←(part)

$16 - 9 = $ ____ and

$16 - 7 = $ ____

Finish the subtraction facts.

5. 9   17  8 $17 - 8 = $ ____ and

$17 - 9 = $ ____

Name _____

Fact Families

Solve two addition and two
subtraction sentences.
Use dot cards and numbers to help.

(part) (part) (whole) | (whole) (part) (part)

1.
15

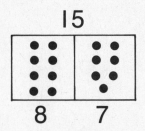

8 7

$8 + 7 = 15$ | $15 - 8 = 7$

$7 + 8 = 15$ | $15 - 7 = 8$

2.
14

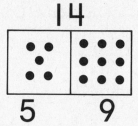

5 9

$5 + 9 = \underline{}$ $14 - 5 = \underline{}$

$9 + 5 = \underline{}$ $14 - 9 = \underline{}$

3.
16

9 7

$9 + 7 = \underline{}$ $16 - 9 = \underline{}$

$7 + 9 = \underline{}$ $16 - 7 = \underline{}$

4.
17

9 8

$9 + 8 = \underline{}$ $17 - 9 = \underline{}$

$8 + 9 = \underline{}$ $17 - 8 = \underline{}$

Using a Number Sentence

Ring the number sentence that fits the story.
Find the answer.
Then ring the rest of the answer.

> Subtract to take away.

1. 6 children are in the sandbox.
2 children went home.
How many stayed?

$6 + 2 =$ ___

$(6 - 2 =$ ___$)$

___ went home.

(stayed in the sandbox.)

---

2. 3 trucks and 2 cars
are in the sandbox.
How many toys are in the sandbox?

> Add to find how many in all.

$3 + 2 =$ ___

$3 - 2 =$ ___

___ toys in all.

___ toys are left.

---

3. There are 7 pails and 3 shovels
in the sandbox.
How many more pails than
shovels are there?

> Subtract to find how many more.

___ pails in all.

$7 + 3 =$ ___

$7 - 3 =$ ___

___ more pails than shovels.

Name _____

Counting On by Ones

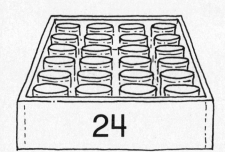 24 25 26 27

$$24 \ + \ 3 \ = \ 27$$

Use blocks. Write the numbers
as you count on. Write the sum.

1.

30   31   32

$$30 + 2 = \rule{1cm}{0.4pt}$$

2.

54   ___   ___

$$54 + 3 = \rule{1cm}{0.4pt}$$

3.

39   ___

$$39 + 1 = \rule{1cm}{0.4pt}$$

4.

42   ___   ___

$$42 + 2 = \rule{1cm}{0.4pt}$$

Making a Ten

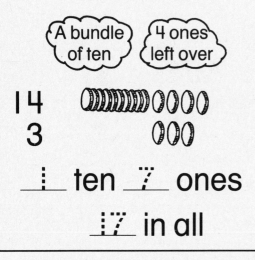

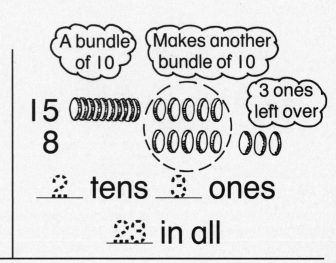

14
3

__1__ ten __7__ ones

__17__ in all

15
8

__2__ tens __3__ ones

__23__ in all

Ring another ten when you can.
How many are there in all?

1. 13
3

___ ten ___ ones

___ in all

18
4

___ tens ___ ones

___ in all

2. 14
5

___ ten ___ ones

___ in all

17
5

___ tens ___ ones

___ in all

Name _____

Understanding the Operations

17 square beads
5 circle beads

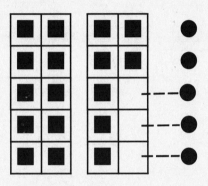

17
+ 5
22

22 beads in all

Count on or use a ⊞ to add. Write the answer.

1. Tanya had 16 stamps.
She got 3 more stamps.
How many stamps does she have in all?

16
+ 3
____

____ stamps

---

2. Greg had 18 baseball cards.
He got 4 more baseball cards.
How many baseball cards does
he have in all?

____
+ ____
____

____ baseball cards

---

3. 25 people were on the bus.
6 more people got on.
How many people are on the bus now?

____
+ ____
____

____ people

Name _____

Counting On by Tens

Count on by tens to add the second number.
Ring the answer. Write the answer.

1. 13
      +30
      43

13	← **Start**
23	← 10 more
33	← 10 more
(43)	← 10 more

2. 26
      +20

26	← **Start**
36	← 10 more
46	← 10 more
56	

3. 32
      +10

| 32 |
| 42 |
| 52 |
| 62 |

4. 17
      +30

| 17 |
| 27 |
| 37 |
| 47 |

5. 24
      +20

| 24 |
| 34 |
| 44 |
| 54 |

6. 18 →
      +10

| 18 |
| |

7. 35 →
      +10

| |
| |

8. 29 →
      +20

| |
| |

Name _____

Adding Tens and Ones

Count the tens and ones.
Write how many in all.

1. 24
  + 13
  ——
   37

  tens ones

2. 46
  + 32
  ——

3. 35
  + 11
  ——

4. 12
  + 43
  ——

Draw tens and ones to show each number.
Write how many in all.

5. 21
  + 15
  ——

6. 42
  + 23
  ——

Name _____

Counting Back by Ones

Count back to find the difference.
Ring the answer.

1.  − 2   26   ⨀25⨀   24   23

ⓛ   ②

2.  − 3   33   32   31   30

3.  − 2   15   14   13   12

4.  − 3   37   36   35   34

5. Write the numbers to count back. Ring the answer.

 − 3   18   ___   ___

Counting Back by Tens

Count back by tens to take away the second number.
Ring the answer. Write the answer.

1. 43
    − 30
    ⌐3⌐

(13)	← 10 less
23	← 10 less
33	← 10 less
43	← Start

2. 36
    − 20

16	← 10 less
26	← 10 less
36	← Start

3. 24
    − 10

| 14 |
| 24 |

4. 45
    − 20

| 25 |
| 35 |
| 45 |

5. 39
    − 20

| 19 |
| 29 |
| 39 |

6. 22
    − 10

| 22 |

7. 37
    − 20

8. 48
    − 20

Name _____

Subtracting Tens and Ones

Cross out tens and ones. Find the difference.

1.

Tens	Ones
2	6
− 1	3
⋮	⊙

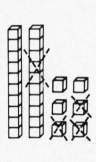

2.

Tens	Ones
3	4
− 1	2

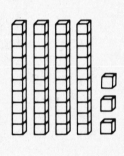

3.

Tens	Ones
3	8
− 2	5

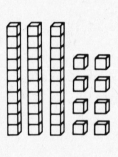

4.

Tens	Ones
4	3
− 1	0

5.

Tens	Ones
4	5
− 2	2

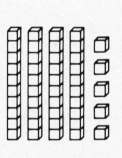

6.

Tens	Ones
5	7
− 3	1

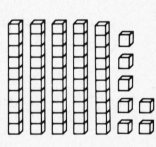

7.
$$55 - 23$$

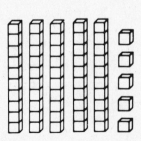

8.
$$69 - 34$$

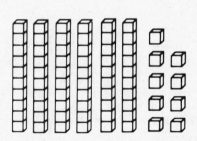

Use with text pages 367 – 368. **RS-1**

Name _____

Choosing a Calculation Method

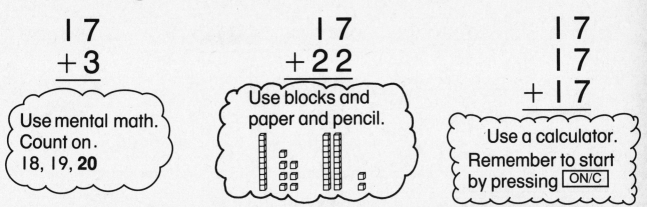

$$\begin{array}{r} 1\,7 \\ +\ 3 \\ \hline \end{array}$$

Use mental math.
Count on.
18, 19, **20**

$$\begin{array}{r} 1\,7 \\ +2\,2 \\ \hline \end{array}$$

Use blocks and
paper and pencil.

$$\begin{array}{r} 1\,7 \\ 1\,7 \\ +\,1\,7 \\ \hline \end{array}$$

Use a calculator.
Remember to start
by pressing ON/C

Use a different calculation method to solve each problem.

1. 24 children on the
yellow bus. 32 children
on the blue bus. How
many children on
both buses?

Use blocks and
paper and pencil.

$$\begin{array}{r} 24 \\ +\ 32 \\ \hline \end{array}$$

_____ children   _____

2. 26 children on the bus.
3 more children got on.
How many children on
the bus now?

Use mental math.

$$\begin{array}{r} 26 \\ +\ 3 \\ \hline \end{array}$$

_____ children   _____

3. 3 buses.
26 children on each bus.
How many children in all?

Use a calculator.

$$\begin{array}{r} 26 \\ 26 \\ +\ 26 \\ \hline \end{array}$$

_____ children   _____

Name _____

Multiplying Equal Groups of Two

3 twos = 6

Use counters to show the wheels.

Count by twos to finish the sentence.

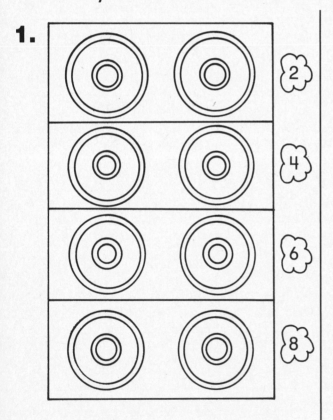

1.

2
4
6
8

4 twos = ____

2.

2
4
____
____
____

5 twos = ____

Name _____

Multiplying Equal Groups of Five

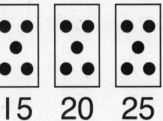

6 fives = 30

5   10   15   20   25   30

Ring each group of 5.
Count by fives. Tell how many.

1.
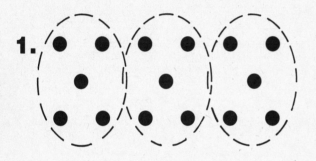

3 fives = ____

2.

4 fives = ____

3.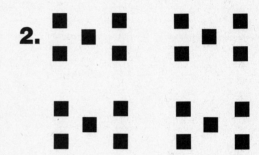

2 fives = ____

4.

5 fives = ____

Understanding the Operations

Color the cubes to show the story.
Finish the subtraction sentence.
Answer the question.

1. Jan made a train with 10 cubes.
6 cubes are red. The rest are blue.
How many cubes are blue?

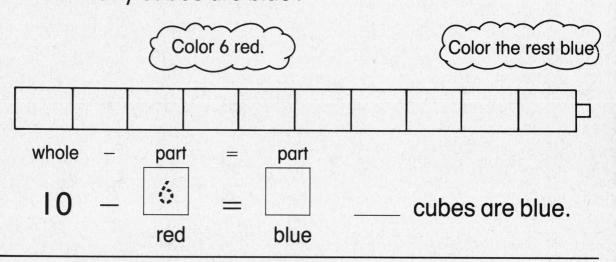

Color 6 red.   Color the rest blue

whole   –   part   =   part

10   – $\boxed{6}$ = $\boxed{}$ ____ cubes are blue.

red   blue

2. Uri made a train with 11 cubes.
4 cubes are red. The rest are blue.
How many cubes are blue?

11   – $\boxed{}$ = $\boxed{}$ ____ cubes are blue.

red   blue

Name _____

Understanding Division: Sharing

Draw lines to make equal groups.
Write how many are in each group.

1.

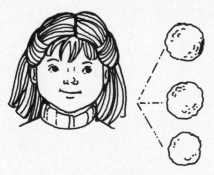 

2 children.   Each gets ___

---

2. 3 children.

Each gets ___ .

3. 2 children.

Each gets ___  .

---

4. 3 children.

Each gets ___ 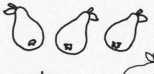 .

Name _____

Understanding Division: Separating

Draw rings to make equal groups.
Write how many groups.

1. 10 marbles   5 in each group

 groups

---

2. 8 marbles   4 in each group

_____ groups

---

3. 12 marbles   3 in each group

_____ groups

Use counters. Show the amount.
Make equal groups. Write how many groups.

4. 16 marbles   **5.** 12 marbles
2 in each group   4 in each group

_____ groups   _____ groups

Name _____

Halves

 $\dfrac{1}{2}$ ← 1 part shaded

← 2 equal parts in all

Write the fraction.

1. 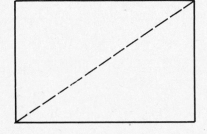 $\dfrac{1}{\boxed{}}$

2. 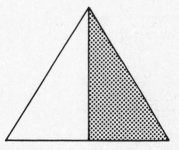 $\dfrac{\boxed{}}{2}$

3. 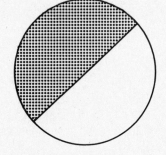 $\dfrac{\boxed{}}{2}$

4. 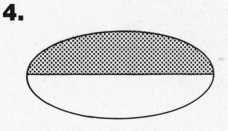 $\dfrac{1}{\boxed{}}$

Color one half. Write the fraction.

5. 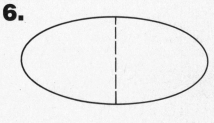 $\dfrac{\boxed{}}{\boxed{}}$

6. 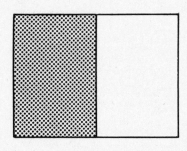 $\dfrac{\boxed{}}{\boxed{}}$

Name _____

Fractions: Thirds and Fourths

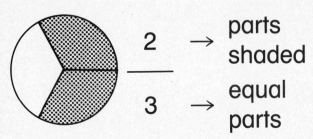 $\dfrac{2}{3}$ → parts shaded / equal parts

two thirds shaded $\dfrac{2}{3}$

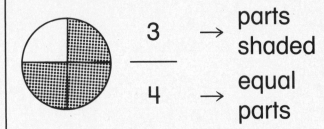 $\dfrac{3}{4}$ → parts shaded / equal parts

three fourths shaded $\dfrac{3}{4}$

Color the shape.   Show how much is shaded.

1. 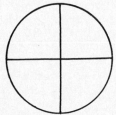 3 parts shaded

three fourths shaded $\dfrac{3}{4}$

2. 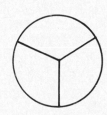 I part shaded

one third shaded $\dfrac{1}{3}$

3. 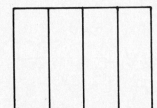 I part shaded

one fourth shaded $\dfrac{1}{4}$

4. 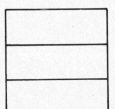 2 parts shaded

two thirds shaded $\dfrac{2}{3}$

5. 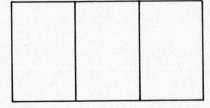 one third shaded $\dfrac{1}{3}$

6. 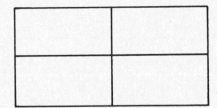 three fourths shaded $\dfrac{3}{4}$

Name _____

Fractions: Using Sets

1. Color $\frac{1}{3}$. ← Color 1 mouse.
    ← _____ mice in all

2. Color $\frac{1}{2}$. ← Color 1 bird.
    ← _____ birds in all

3. Color $\frac{1}{2}$.

4. Color $\frac{2}{3}$.

5. Color $\frac{1}{4}$.

6. Color $\frac{1}{2}$.

Finding Missing Data

Solve. Use the data from the fruit bins to help.

1. Jeff bought an orange for 20¢ and a banana. How much did he spend?

He spent ____ ¢.

```
    20
 +  10
 ─────
    30
```

First, write the data you know. The orange costs 20¢.

Next, look on the bin to find the data you need. The banana costs 10¢.

Finally, add to find the total.

Write the answer.

2. Sue bought a peach for 25¢ and an apple. How much did she spend?

```
    ____
 +  ____
 ─────
    ____
```

She spent ____ ¢.

3. Manuel bought a tangerine for 10¢ and a pear. How much did he spend?

```
    ____
 +  ____
 ─────
    ____
```

He spent ____ ¢.